Fodor's Guide to The Da Vinci Code

Edited by Jennifer Paull & Christopher Culwell

Photography by Vanessa Berberian

D0957206

Fodor's

Editors' Note

IF YOU'RE AMONG THE MILLIONS of readers who have been fascinated by *The Da Vinci Code* and are eager to know more about the world of the novel, this is the book for you. Following the path of Robert Langdon and Sophie Neveu, we'll take you deeper into the mystery by discussing the locations, people, historic events, and symbols involved in the story. With photos, maps, and fun, expert essays, *Fodor's Guide to* The Da Vinci Code will amplify your experience of the novel. And it's a thrilling read in its own right. Enjoy!

Jennifer Paull and Christopher Culwell

Contents

MAPS & FLOOR PLANS

paris

A Shocking Night at the Ritz

RENOWNED SYMBOLOGY SCHOLAR Robert Langdon gets a wee-hours wake-up call from a French police agent. (Not even the Ritz Paris staff can turn away the Police Judiciare.) The Ritz is right in the heart of things, just a few blocks from that enormous art treasure-house, the Louvre.

THE RITZ PARIS

Ever since Swiss hotelier César Ritz opened the doors of this, his first eponymous hotel, in 1898, the mere name of this venerable institution has been synonymous with luxury. Things are done here on a grand scale, as a sleepy Langdon relays in the opening pages of *The Da Vinci Code*. He slowly surveys his surroundings: posh robe with Ritz monogram, frescoed walls, antique furniture.

And that was probably only a junior suite. The hotel also offers more palatial suites, bearing the names of famous Ritz residents past and present: the Coco Chanel, the Marcel Proust, and the Elton John. Former Ritz regular Ernest Hemingway is, fittingly, celebrated with a bar (*see* the Hemingway Bar sidebar *below*).

Now the turn-of-the-20th-century indulgences are matched with modern amenities, though the latter are sometimes camouflaged as the former. Need to summon a valet or maid? Just use the gold pull chain above your marble bath. The television, meanwhile, may be built into a gleaming mirror.

You could easily spend days prowling the hotel's palatial interior, filled with shops, gardens, bars, clubs, restaurants, a famed cooking school, and a subterranean health club and spa. In the health club's expansive, opulent pool, you can even swim with a symbol of feminine power and mystery: mosaic mermaids decorate the shallow end.

Amenities aside, one of the Ritz's biggest advantages is its location on the stately, 17th-century place Vendôme, within easy walking distance of many of the city's key sights. This centrality comes into play at the end of the *Code*, when Langdon walks out into place Vendôme and quickly on to the Louvre. If he hadn't been in such a hurry, he might have paused to size up the column commissioned in 1806 by Napoleon (that's the emperor on top, in a toga). The column celebrates the French victory at Austerlitz over the Russians and Austrians. Cannons captured at the battle were melted down to wrap the column in bronze.

The Ritz is a landmark in its own right, with its victories in hospitality and culinary innovations. Ritz introduced many comforts now taken for granted, such as double-glazed windows, improved ventilation, walk-in wardrobes, and bathrooms in every guest room. He purposely chose soft, indirect lighting and peach-colored robes to flatter guests' complexions. And in another prescient move, he tapped the formidably talented chef, Provence-born Auguste Escoffier, as head chef of his hotels. Together, they catered to the rich and famous; they even shook up social mores a bit. At the time, upper-crust women did not go out in public without their husbands or chaperones, but the Ritz's genteel tea room became an acceptable place for ladies to meet unchaperoned. Little wonder high society women flocked to the hotel.

While Ritz advanced the state of hospitality, Escoffier likewise introduced numerous innovations in the kitchen, emphasizing seasonal dishes, lighter sauces, fewer courses, and simpler presentations. He also revolutionized the system of labor in the kitchen, eliminating some of the independent fiefdoms—which slowed preparation, duplicated effort, and compromised quality—in favor of having multiple cooks contribute toward a finished dish, which the head chef then approved before it was served. Today his approach reigns in top kitchens all over the world.

Fittingly, the Ritz now offers instruction in the mystic arts—not of symbology, but of cooking. Take one of the Ritz-Escoffier

The Hemingway Bar

*L*ong before *The Da Vinci Code*, the Ritz Paris was a fixture in the world of belles lettres, frequented by such masters as Marcel Proust and F. Scott Fitzgerald. The hotel's most famous writer-patron, however, was arguably Ernest Hemingway.

Hemingway's legendary association with the Ritz Paris dates from the Liberation of 1944. On August 25, 1944, he pulled up to the hotel's rue Cambon entrance in a Jeep, then strode in at the head of a group of soldiers and "liberated" the joint by doing his best to drain the wine cellar. (Reportedly they began with the premiers crus, which the manager had successfully hidden from the Germans.)

The Ritz would become a recurring element in Hemingway's life. He once said of the hotel, "You must come here hoping for forgetfulness, for meetings, for discoveries." Those were fitting words. After the Liberation, working out of room 31, Hemingway began a relationship with war correspondent Mary Welsh, who was staying in room 86. Soon, Hemingway's third marriage fell apart; Welsh became his fourth and final wife.

Here too, the story goes, a trunk full of notes on his first years in Paris turned up in the 1950s, giving him the raw material to write his memoir *A Moveable Feast*. In it, he recounts drinking in the 1920s at the Ritz's Bar Cambon, also known as Frank's, for Frank Meier, the bartender. Many years later, Frank's successor, Georges Scheuer, asked Hemingway about the author every tourist wanted to hear about: F. Scott Fitzgerald. "He wrote two very good books and . . . some good short stories," Hemingway recounted. Did he frequent this bar often? asked Scheuer. "It meant very much to him," said Hemingway.

The namesake bar's decor salutes Papa. Its walls are lined with 25 photographs taken by Hemingway of inspirational locales, tapas are served in honor of his time in Spain, and cigar nights are held on Wednesdays. Beyond the Hemingway connection, the bar succeeds in its own right, primarily through the skills of Colin Field. Clad in a crisp white jacket, Field adorns his drinks with orchids, roses, or fruit.

Would Hemingway approve of the bar's semiformal dress code? Surely it wouldn't stop him. After all, this was the man who said, "When I dream of afterlife in heaven, the action always takes place at the Paris Ritz."

School of Gastronomy's master classes or courses in French bread baking or *viennoiserie* (pastry) making. The school's goal is to make good on Escoffier's mantra: "Good cuisine is the foundation of true happiness." ✉ *15 pl. Vendôme, Louvre/Tuileries, 1er arrondissement, 01–43–16–36–68, www.ritzparis.com.* Ⓜ *Opéra.*

PJ: WE'RE TALKING POLICE, NOT PAJAMAS

Found a bloody, naked corpse contorted in a symbolic position on the parquet floors of the Louvre? Enter the DCPJ.

In *The Da Vinci Code*, the job of solving the mysterious death of the curator Jacques Saunière ostensibly falls to the DCPJ, or Direction Centrale Police Judiciare, the central branch of the Judiciary Police. In the novel's opening pages, Langdon is first summoned by a DCPJ lieutenant, then delivered to Captain Bezu Fache to "assist" with the investigation.

Although Langdon likens the DCPJ to the U.S. FBI, much of the French organization is actually more akin to a police detective squad. According to criminology researcher Jacques Borricand, the DCPJ—or the PJ, as the French typically call it—"is in charge of coordinating the search for the most dangerous delinquents and the investigation of the most serious offenses."

With a mandate like that, it's no wonder the PJ has stormed popular culture. The French love a good *policier*, or police drama, and indeed the PJ has been the subject of many films, television episodes, and books. Just take the popular French weekly television show, *P.J.* It's like *NYPD Blue,* only set in Paris.

The DCPJ itself was founded in the beginning of the 20th century. Its Paris headquarters are on the Ile de la Cité at 36 quai des Orfèvres. (The address is sometimes used as shorthand for the PJ, such as in the 2004 French film titled *36, Quai des Orfèvres.*) The central location, poised between the city's left and right banks, was especially useful in the days when inspectors caught cabs to crime scenes.

Of course, the PJ doesn't work alone. France has two different police forces. The prefect-based Police Nationale has four branches (one of which is the DCPJ) and includes your typical *flic* (cop): traffic cops, detectives, plus the feared Compagnies Républicaines de Sécurité (riot cops). Then there's the Gendarmerie Nationale, a paramilitary force responsible for security at airports, borders, and in rural areas.

In the popular imagination, however, the PJ is perhaps most famously associated with Inspector Jules Maigret, the fictional Paris PJ detective created by Georges Simenon, a crime reporter turned prolific author. Beginning in 1931, Simenon wrote 75 Maigret novels in 40 years. Maigret is the French answer to Sherlock Holmes; rather than just focus on the identity of the perpetrator, he's equally interested in the psychology behind the crime. Criminals, beware.

THE TUILERIES GARDENS

As Langdon is driven through the Tuileries Gardens at the start of the novel, he muses that he reveres them because of their connection to the birth of Impressionism. Parisians hold the park in high esteem too, for its history, its museums, and its tranquil beauty.

It wasn't always so beautiful though. The gardens, as Dan Brown explains, take their name from the red roof tiles that were once made here. The area was a big pit; clay was dug on-site, shaped into tiles, and fired in kilns (*les tuileries*). To get an idea of their shape, order some *tuiles* in a Paris bakery—they're delicious sugar cookies shaped in a tile-like curve.

In the *Code*, Langdon is driven from the Ritz down rue Castiglione, straight across rue de Rivoli into the Tuileries. Don't try to copy his route in a car—you can only get in on foot.

The gated entrance on rue Castiglione leads to a path reserved for dog walkers—watch your step! The second green gate leads into the main gardens. In traditional French style, the Tuileries is lined with neatly trimmed trees and punctuated with sculptures. And it has two perfectly round fountains, complete with big-mouthed carp waiting for bread.

In summer, the stretch of the Tuileries nearest rue de Rivoli is sometimes filled with amusement park rides. (Keep an eye out for small children covered in cotton candy, which is called *barbe-à-papa*, "daddy's beard.") And for a couple of weeks in spring and fall, long white Fashion Week tents appear, as chic and outrageous fashionistas strut along the garden's paths. For a few special nights in August, an outdoor cinema is set up. There are also cafés in the Tuileries, for a lovely break any time of year.

Facing place de la Concorde at one end of the gardens are two small yet not-to-be-missed museums. The Musée du Jeu de Paume hosts splashy photography exhibits. The matching building nearer the Seine is the Musée de l'Orangerie, due to reopen in 2006 after years of renovation. Here you'll find the largest versions of Claude Monet's *Water Lilies*. It's a perfect location for these great Impressionist works; as Langdon reflects during his drive, Monet worked in these gardens. Edouard Manet and Auguste Renoir also enthusiastically set up their easels in the Tuileries.

The two museums are leftovers from the Tuileries Palace. As you walk towards the Louvre, imagine a fourth wall, enclosing the pyramid. The now-demolished Tuileries Palace was built in 1564 by Catherine de' Medici, but she didn't stay long. A fortune-teller predicted she would die near St-Germain and since the Tuileries is in the parish of St-Germain, Catherine quickly packed her bags and moved out. Over the next two hundred years, the palace was largely neglected. André Le Nôtre (*see* the sidebar *below*) gave it an elaborate garden but Louis XIV disliked the palace and moved out to Versailles. Eventually, during the early months of the Revolution, King Louis XVI was forced back into this Paris palace. From the Tuileries, the desperate royal family made their botched escape. Riots broke out, the royal guards were massacred, and Le Nôtre's serene gardens were littered with 1,000 gruesome corpses.

After the Revolution, Napoleon took back the Tuileries as a royal Paris residence; Napoleon III also lived in the palace. But in 1870, the imperial family fled—Empress Eugénie literally snuck out a back door in disguise, to escape a gathering mob—and the following year, the palace was burned during one of the Commune battles. It was never rebuilt. Today, a tiny piece of the Tuileries Palace remains at the furthest edge of the Louvre's Grand Gallery.

With the Tuileries Palace demolished, the Louvre took shape as we see it today. The uneven U-shape of the main museum stands with opened arms reaching towards the gardens. If you pause un-

André Le Nôtre's "Green Geometry"

orticultural historians have observed that the truly stylish French garden of the late 1600s controlled nature while extolling its virtues. Sounds like beauty-column advice, but at the time it was a breakthrough in landscape design.

The garden as an imitation of unruly nature was all the rage until 1650, when Nicholas Fouquet, Louis XIV's ill-fated minister of finance, unveiled the 1,500-meter-long spread at his château, Vaux-le-Vicomte. If the horticultural arts ever had a watershed moment, this was it. The green thumb at Vaux was André Le Nôtre (1613–1700), the unassuming son of the superintendent of the Tuileries Gardens and a student of optics and perspective. Fouquet charged Le Nôtre with the task of designing a grand park that would compliment but not upstage his stupendous château. To this end, Le Nôtre divided the park in two equal parts along a central axis with the château at the center, making it the focal point of the park. The meandering paths and hidden nooks of yore were replaced by a "green geometry," a flat vista of gravel paths, lagoons, multicolored parterres, and clever punctuations of statues and fountains. The arrangement of elements was such that it focused the eye on the horizon, creating the illusion of an expanse that was both limitless yet fathomable in a single glance.

The result may look like it's all about harmony and geometry, but it's also an exercise in power. Indeed, as art historian Robert I.C. Fisher has written, "At Vaux, your eye stretches along nearly two miles of manicured gardens before it finally comes up against a wall of trees. The end result: the entire world seems within grasp, controlled, and ordered."

Order on such a scale appealed to Louis XIV, who made Le Nôtre his royal gardener, entrusting to him such major projects as the grounds at Versailles, Fontainebleau, the Champs-Elysées, and the Tuileries. Le Nôtre honed his penchant for geometry and optical illusion on all of these assignments, creating a trend in French landscaping that earned him no end of commissions and a great many imitators. Indeed, the garden as limitless expanse was a look that eventually found its way across the Channel and around the globe, holding sway well into the next century, until the British taste for Palladian style brought a return to unfussy naturalism.

derneath the Arc du Carrousel, you can admire an incredible, slightly-off-center, vista: a sight line runs from the Louvre's pyramid through the Arc and down the paths of the Tuileries. If you look past the Tuileries trees, your eye will travel up the Champs-Elysées, through the Arc de Triomphe, and towards the third archway of La Défense.

ARC DU CARROUSEL

It's fair to say that Napoleon was a little man with a taste for big monuments. The Arc du Carrousel was commissioned in 1806 to commemorate Napoleon's victory at Austerlitz the previous year. The arch's design is based on the Arch of Septimius Severus in Rome. Napoleon was awfully fond of his Roman-style monuments, not least because he considered himself to be recreating the grandeur of Rome in 19th-century Paris.

The arch is 63 feet high, 75 feet wide, and 24 feet deep, decorated with rose and white marble from the Languedoc region. On top perch statues of Victory and Peace with a chariot pulled by four horses. The horses that first crowned the arch were taken from the Basilica of San Marco in Venice. These were returned after Napoleon's fall from power, and eventually replaced with copies. The chariot now holds a female figure representing the Restoration of the Bourbon monarchy.

The Arc du Carrousel takes its name from the equestrian processions and jousting tournaments that once took place on the site. Louis XIV, always a fan of pomp and circumstance, held a huge fancy-dress party on this spot in 1662. Louis himself, dressed as an ancient Roman, paraded with other members of the nobility gussied up as Persians, Turks, and Indians. These days, you'll probably see a truly international crowd milling around the archway, taking in one of the city's most spectacular views down the Champs-Elysées.

Murder at the Louvre

ARRIVING AT THE LOUVRE MUSEUM, Langdon meets the police captain, Bezu Fache. The intimidating captain takes him to the Denon Wing, where the body of curator Jacques Saunière lies splayed out on the floor. All around hang masterpieces of Italian Renaissance painting, including works by Raphael, Caravaggio, and the mysterious genius, Leonardo da Vinci.

THE LOUVRE'S HISTORY

Long before Langdon sets foot in the Louvre, this former royal palace turned art museum was a place of mystery, intrigue, and murder.

The Louvre began as a fortress on the outskirts of Paris in the 1190s. King Philippe Auguste (1180–1223), who had the English breathing rather uncomfortably down his neck from Normandy, decided to build defensive walls around the city of Paris. The Louvre was the western anchor of those walls, as well as a convenient place to collect taxes on trade moving up and down the Seine. With an inner tower protected by a deep moat, the Louvre soon became the model for medieval fortifications throughout France. The tower was used to house the royal treasury and arms, as well as a few unlucky prisoners. The king lived elsewhere, probably safe behind the walls on the Ile de la Cité.

The Louvre became a royal palace under Charles V (1337–1380). Around the original fortress he created a fairy-tale castle, complete with turrets, grand staircases, and lavish entertainments for the nobility.

The Pastiche Palace

The building we know today was begun by François I (1494–1547) in 1546. François was a keen patron of the arts, particularly impressed with the recent flowering of Renaissance Italy. The new Louvre was his way of keeping up with the Joneses. He invited many well-known Italian artists to work in France, including, most famously, Leonardo da Vinci.

François died a few months after work began, and his son, Henri II, took over. Their architect, Pierre Lescot, continued building in the Renaissance style, and you can clearly see the 16th-century fashion for all things Greek and Roman in the Salle des Caryatides, Henri's reception hall. It is named for the monumental statues that hold up the musician's gallery. They are carved to look like the ruins of classical statues—missing arms and all.

The history of the Louvre, indeed the history of France, would read quite differently if it weren't for certain royal mothers—particularly Catherine de' Medici. Daughter of the powerful Florentine banking family, wife of Henri II, and regent through the reigns of her two sons (François II and Charles IX), she was the mastermind behind one of the bloodiest episodes ever to take place at the Louvre, the St. Bartholomew's Day Massacre.

In a token effort to end the wars between Catholics and Protestants (Huguenots) that raged throughout France, Catherine decided to marry off her daughter, Marguerite de Valois, to the Protestant Henri de Navarre. Many of France's powerful Protestants gathered in Paris for the festivities. On August 24th, 1572, five days after the wedding, the bells of the royal parish church at St-Germain-l'Auxerrois raised the alarm to begin the massacre of the Huguenots. Henri escaped inside the Louvre with his bride, while his entourage was slaughtered in the courtyards below.

Henri de Navarre returned to the Louvre as Henri IV of France in 1594, as a converted Catholic. His is the famous remark "Paris is worth a mass." He initiated an ambitious renovation of the Louvre, including the completion of the Grand Gallery along the Seine. The Grand Gallery now displays the Louvre's world-famous collection of Italian paintings. Despite his popularity during his reign, *"le bon roi Henri"* (good King Henry) met a bad end. He was stabbed to death by a Catholic fanatic in 1610.

After the death of Henri IV, his second wife, Marie de' Medici (watch out for those Medici women!) became regent for her son Louis XIII. Her personal and political exploits are immortalized in a series of 24 paintings by Flemish artist Peter Paul Rubens. These puffy, aggrandizing works now hang in the Louvre's Richelieu Wing.

When Louis XIV (1638–1715) took the reins of government in 1661, he had a deep suspicion of Paris's unruly inhabitants. To keep an eye on the rebellious nobility, Louis had to centralize his court. He picked up on Henri IV's grand plan for the Louvre, quadrupling the size of the Cour Carrée (the courtyard directly behind the Louvre's main façade) and creating the opulent Galerie d'Apollon. This heavily gilded gallery was a dry run for the over-the-top aesthetics of his palace at Versailles.

In the 1660s, Louis XIV's minister Jean-Baptiste Colbert founded the royal academies of art, architecture, letters, and sciences. This was the beginning of the Louvre as a home for living artists. In 1699, the annual exhibition of the Royal Academy of Painting and Sculpture moved from the nearby Palais Royal to the Grand Gallery of the Louvre. In 1725, the exhibition moved to the Louvre's Salon Carré—hence the name *salon* for the fashionable painting exhibitions that were the talk of Paris right up until the Impressionists shook things up in the 1880s.

When the royal court left town for Versailles in the late 1600s, the Louvre became the world's grandest artists' squat. The academies of arts and sciences hummed with activity, and selections from the royal collection were used for lectures and training.

Although the Louvre was in the hands of the academics, the art was still reserved for a select population. But there was increasing talk in favor of a permanent public painting exhibition in the Grand Gallery. When Louis XVI (1754–1793) came to power in 1774, he appointed Charles-Claude de Flahaut, Comte de la Billarderie d'Angivillier, as Director General of Royal Buildings. D'Angivillier made the creation of a public museum within the Louvre his pet project, but it would take the French Revolution of 1789 to complete the transformation of the Louvre from a royal stronghold to the people's palace.

Off With Their Heads: A Royal Collection Goes Public

During the guillotine spree that followed the French Revolution, the royal art collection was effectively nationalized. The transfer of these rare and precious objects into the hands of the republic was a powerful symbol of the new order.

Louis XVI was executed in January of 1793. On August 10, 1793 the Musée Central des Arts opened in the Grand Gallery with an exhibition of 538 works from the former royal collections. The show included many of the crowd-pleasers that still hang today, among them Raphael's *La Belle Jardinière* and of course, the *Mona Lisa*.

Creating a public museum also meant creating a museum-going public. Even the labels proved confusing for the early viewers. Busts of Plato and Alexander the Great were mistaken for portraits of the Duc de Brissac and the Prince de Condé, their former aristocratic owners.

There was no admission charge until 1922; the only qualification was to be "decently dressed." Nevertheless, the museum's visitors were a motley crew. Tramps came to warm themselves by the stoves, and young women painters, barred from the traditional art academies, came to copy, socialize—and flirt.

When Napoleon declared himself emperor in 1804, in one of his signature egomaniacal flourishes, he renamed the Louvre the Musée Napoleon. Since he conveniently installed various relatives as kings, princes, and dukes of Italy, he and his chief curator Dominique Vivant Denon (*see* the Denon sidebar *below*) could go shopping among Italy's art treasures.

Bringing these "lifted" works to Paris was part of Napoleon's PR machine. By adding to the collections of the Louvre he hoped to boost France's reputation as a cultural as well as military giant. World-famous sculptures, including the *Laocoön* and the *Apollo Belvedere* from the Vatican, were paraded around Paris on flower-laden floats, accompanied by imperialist ditties: *La Grèce les céda, Rome les a perdu / leur sort changea deux fois, il ne changera plus* ("Greece gave them up, Rome lost them too / their lot has changed two times, it will not change anew"). Many of these works were returned soon after 1815, when Napoleon was deposed.

But the Louvre didn't stop growing. Even during the governmental upheavals of the 19th century, the museum managed to expand its holdings, going farther afield to gather material. In 1843, Emile Bota, a French diplomat working in Mosul (in what is now Iraq), discovered fragments from the palace of the Assyrian king Sargon II dating from the 8th century B.C. The huge winged guardian figures were a hit with the public when King Louis-Philippe opened an Assyrian museum within the Louvre in 1847.

The artists who revolutionized early-20th-century art spent a lot of time in the Louvre. Henri Matisse went to the Louvre to copy its old masters as part of his training—and also because young artists could often sell the copies to the museum to supplement their meager incomes. The Louvre never bought a copy from Matisse, though, because his works were never faithful enough to the originals!

The museum's most precious holdings made it through World War II by going underground. In late August 1939, the Louvre's most important works were packed up and evacuated to hiding places in châteaux throughout France with the help of trucks borrowed from Samaritaine, the nearby department store.

The Pyramid Scheme

François Mitterand, the president of France from 1981 to 1995, is the most recent leader to leave his mark on the Louvre. His *grands travaux* ("great works") for the city of Paris included an overhaul of the city's major cultural institutions. Under this impetus rose La Grande Pyramide, the crowning glory of his controversial renovation of the Louvre.

To complete the transformation of the Louvre from a royal residence to a modern mega-museum, Mitterand commissioned the Chinese-American architect I. M. Pei. Pei's challenge was to make the Louvre more user-friendly. Past architects were more concerned with glorifying the kings of France—they could never have imagined welcoming the more than 7 million people a year who currently visit the museum. To keep the foot traffic flowing, Pei proposed a huge central entrance hall topped with a 70-foot-high glass pyramid. The pyramid would act as a giant skylight, illuminating the previously untapped basement space. Pei also carved out a huge underground shopping mall that runs from the main pyramid to the Arc du Carrousel. This space now houses the Louvre's gift shops, a food court, a conference center—even a Virgin

Megastore. At the entrance to the commercial shopping mall is the inverted pyramid.

The other major piece of Pei's project was to reclaim the Richelieu Wing as exhibition space for the Louvre. Until 1981, the wing facing the rue de Rivoli served as the French Ministry of Finance (the Cour Napoleon, where the pyramid now stands, was their parking lot). Mitterand moved the bureaucrats out and let Pei redesign the wing for exhibition space. With this addition, the Louvre became the largest art museum in the world.

When Pei presented his project to French officials and journalists, the outcry was immediate and vicious—jeers, laughter, and shouts of "This is not Dallas" were heard in the room. The insults flew so thick and fast that the translator finished mute and in tears.

Despite popular opposition, the project went ahead as planned. Building the pyramid was a technological as well as an aesthetic challenge. Pei wanted perfectly transparent glass, not the normal green tinged glass that would give the pyramid the look of "a giant Coke bottle." A new kind of glass was invented especially for the project. There are actually 673, not a satanic 666, panes in the central pyramid.

Before Pei could dig underneath the Louvre, there was some archaeological housekeeping to be done. The foundations of the medieval Louvre, including Philippe Auguste's famous tower, were excavated and are now open to the public on the lower ground floor of the Sully Wing. The building was not the only thing that got a makeover—the museum guards got sleek new uniforms designed by Balenciaga.

The pyramid was inaugurated in 1989, and the Richelieu Wing in 1993, just in time for the bicentennial of the public museum. The French have since come around and La Grande Pyramide is the new symbol of Paris, worthy of the T-shirts and key chains that were once reserved for the Eiffel Tower. Walking past the pyramid at sunset, you can see the old building through the prism of the new. As it has since the Middle Ages, the Louvre has reinvented itself—this time as a museum for the 21st century.

Visiting the Louvre

01-40-20-53-17 for information, www.louvre.fr. Ⓜ *Palais-Royal.*

The Grande Pyramide is the museum's main entry point. To get into the galleries, you may have to wait in two lines: one outside

Napoleon's Eye: Dominique Vivant Denon

Artist, curator, author, and man about town, Dominique Vivant Denon's place in history was fixed by his reputation as "the eye of Napoleon." Napoleon and Denon first crossed paths at the artistic soirées of Madame de Beauharnais, later to become Napoleon's first wife, Josephine. Denon then accompanied Napoleon on his infamous campaign to Egypt. The lavishly illustrated memoir of Denon's travels was a best seller on a *Da Vinci Code* scale.

Napoleon tapped Denon to be the director of the Louvre in 1802. During his tenure, Denon's goal was to make the Louvre the repository of world culture. The fact that he had his pick of war booty from Napoleon's military victories certainly made his job easier. In 1805 he began a series of trips to Italy, Spain, Austria and Germany, visiting the collections of newly conquered territories, making precise inventories and hand-picking works to be sent back to Paris. Among the works he chose were paintings by Fra Angelico, Giotto, and Mantegna—then called the Italian Primitives—giving the Louvre an important lead-up to the Renaissance collections.

His work bringing exotic cultures to the Louvre spilled over into the fashionable decorative arts of the period, since he also controlled Gobelins and Sèvres, the royal tapestry and porcelain factories. By bringing the styles of ancient Greece, Rome, and Egypt out of the museum and into the homes of the wealthy bourgeoisie, Denon ensured the Pottery Barn–like ubiquity of his personal taste.

Baron Denon in 1808.

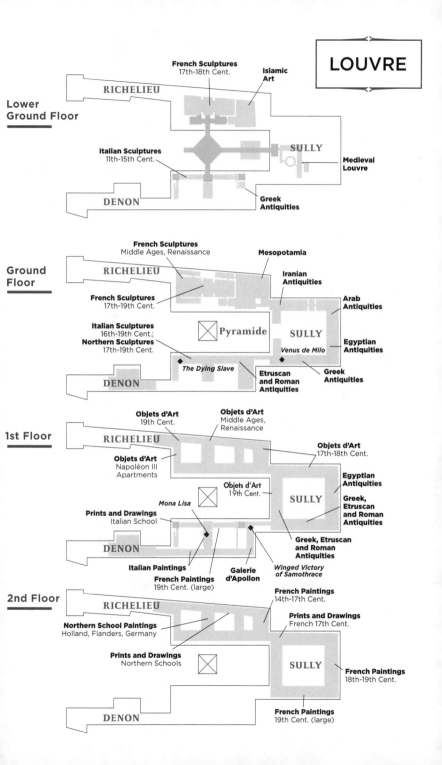

LOUVRE

Lower Ground Floor

RICHELIEU

French Sculptures
17th-18th Cent.

Islamic Art

Italian Sculptures
11th-15th Cent.

SULLY

Medieval Louvre

DENON

Greek Antiquities

Ground Floor

French Sculptures
Middle Ages, Renaissance

RICHELIEU

Mesopotamia

Iranian Antiquities

French Sculptures
17th-19th Cent.

Arab Antiquities

Italian Sculptures
16th-19th Cent.;
Northern Sculptures
17th-19th Cent.

Pyramide

SULLY

Venus de Milo

Egyptian Antiquities

The Dying Slave

DENON

Etruscan and Roman Antiquities

Greek Antiquities

1st Floor

Objets d'Art
19th Cent.

Objets d'Art
Middle Ages, Renaissance

RICHELIEU

Objets d'Art
17th-18th Cent.

Objets d'Art
Napoléon III Apartments

Objets d'Art
19th Cent.

Mona Lisa

Egyptian Antiquities

Prints and Drawings
Italian School

SULLY

Greek, Etruscan and Roman Antiquities

DENON

Greek, Etruscan and Roman Antiquities

Italian Paintings

French Paintings
19th Cent. (large)

Galerie d'Apollon

Winged Victory of Samothrace

2nd Floor

RICHELIEU

French Paintings
14th-17th Cent.

Prints and Drawings
French 17th Cent.

Northern School Paintings
Holland, Flanders, Germany

Prints and Drawings
Northern Schools

SULLY

French Paintings
18th-19th Cent.

DENON

French Paintings
19th Cent. (large)

DENON WING

Nike of Samothrace

Venus and the Three Graces
Botticelli

St. Francis of Assisi Receiving The Stigmata
Giotto

St. Sebastian
Mantegna

The Annunciation
Leonardo da Vinci & Lorenzo di Credi

Oath of the Horatii
David

Coronation of Napoleon
David

Madame Récamier
David

Odalisque
Ingres

The Coronation of the Virgin
Tintoretto

Liberty Guiding the People
Delacroix

The Raft of the Medusa
Géricault

Mona Lisa
Leonardo da Vinci

Salle des Etats

Salon Carré

Bacchus (St. John in the Desert)
Leonardo da Vinci

La Belle Ferronnière
Leonardo da Vinci

St. John the Baptist
Leonardo da Vinci

The Madonna of the Rocks
Leonardo da Vinci

The Wedding Feast at Cana
Veronese

Holy Family
Leonardo da Vinci

Portrait of Baldassare Castiglione
Raphael

Death of the Virgin
Caravaggio

Grand Gallery

the Pyramide entrance and another downstairs at the ticket booths. To shorten the wait, try the alternate entrance in the underground mall, the Carrousel du Louvre, where you can buy entry passes at automatic ticket machines. Be sure to hold onto your ticket; it will get you in to any and all wings as many times as you like during one day. Once inside, stop by the information desk in the main lobby to pick up a free color-coded map.

If you're planning to spend just a few hours in the museum, consider an evening visit. On Wednesday and Friday the Louvre stays open until 9:45 p.m., and on those days the admission fee is a few euros cheaper after 6 p.m. The museum is closed on Tuesday.

THE DENON WING

When Langdon enters the darkened Grand Gallery he is experiencing every tourist's dream—to be nearly alone in the most popular part of the Louvre.

The wing of the Louvre closest to the river Seine, the Denon Wing is named for Dominique Vivant, Baron de Denon, the director of the Louvre under Napoleon. It contains the museum's big three: the *Mona Lisa*, the *Venus de Milo*, and the *Nike of Samothrace* (also called *Winged Victory*). Climbing the grand marble staircase in high tourist season can feel like being in Times Square on New Year's Eve, crowds jostling for a better photo opportunity.

At approximately 1,500 feet long, the Grand Gallery dominates this wing. About a third of the way down the gallery is the newly renovated Salle des Etats, home to both the Louvre's largest painting, Veronese's *The Wedding Feast at Cana* (7 x 10 meters), and its most famous, the *Mona Lisa*. The Louvre's five other works by Leonardo cluster on the wall of the Grand Gallery just outside the Salle des Etats.

Before the Grand Gallery was given over to art, it was used by the royal family as both a rumpus room and a reception hall. The young Louis XIII liked to walk his pet camel up and down the narrow gallery. Later the king, who was a ballet enthusiast, would squeeze in audiences of up to 4,000 for all-night parties and performances.

The Grand Gallery was also the site of Louis XIII's revival of the medieval *cérémonie des écrouelles*, the practice of the king laying hands on the sick. This carefully choreographed ceremony allowed the public to file through the Grand Gallery on particular feast days and receive benediction from the king much as they would from a priest. These blessings helped to reinforce the divine right of kings—the idea that the royalty of France received their power directly from God.

By far the most important events to take place in the Grand Gallery and the connecting Salon Carré were the yearly salons, temporary art exhibitions mounted each year from 1699 to the 1880s to show off new talent. The salon was a testing ground for new artistic styles and a great place to push the envelope of social and sexual mores. At the salon of 1865, Edouard Manet scandalized the critics with his *Olympia* (now in the Musée d'Orsay), a painting of a reclining naked woman modelled after famous nudes by Titian and Velázquez. Instead of tactfully depicting Venus, the mythical goddess of love, Manet dared to paint a common prostitute receiving flowers from one of her wealthy clients. The painting caused such a scandal that it had to be removed after only three days on display.

Today, a walk through the Salon Carré and down the Grand Gallery is a trip through the history of Italian painting. If you follow Langdon's path over the herringbone design of the parquet floor, you can trace the flowering of the Italian Renaissance and beyond—all the way from Cimabue to Caravaggio. And there is indeed a men's room at the far end of the gallery—but the soap there doesn't come in bars like the one Sophie used to trick the police.

Caravaggio's *Virgin*

When dying curator Jacques Saunière yanks a painting off the wall of the Grand Gallery in order to bring security gates crashing down, he seizes one of three Caravaggio paintings hanging in this space. Dan Brown does not specifically name which one, but based on the novel's description, the painting in question is most likely Caravaggio's *The Death of the Virgin*. This tour de force depicts the Apostles and Mary Magdalene witnessing the Virgin Mary's Assumption into heaven.

There are few holier moments in art than the Assumption, especially in Roman Catholic countries like Italy, where the cult of the Madonna overshadows even that of her son Jesus. But while Caravaggio's subject is divine, his work is also intensely irreverent. Indeed, this theatrical staging of the Assumption might have had some down-and-dirty connections. Caravaggio was famous for finding inspiration in the streets outside his door in Rome (and later in Naples). Scholars generally believe that he often used prostitutes as models for his depictions of Christian saints and holy martyrs. And one of art history's more frequently told tales is that the Virgin in *The Death of the Virgin* was based on the artist's studies of the body of a woman who had drowned in the Tiber.

The painting's death scene shows the Virgin as a barefoot woman, faceup on a bed and surrounded by grieving mourners. The figure seated at her feet is probably Mary Magdalene. The Madonna's feet are dirty, and nothing about her depiction by Caravaggio suggests that she is anything but mortal. She wears a red dress, a color typically used for the clothing of the Magdalene. (The Madonna is usually depicted in soothing shades of blue.) In essence, Caravaggio has brought the Virgin back to earth—hardly your standard rendition of the triumph of divine glory over death.

The beauty of the piece is Caravaggio's exquisite rendering of textures and his signature use of chiaroscuro, or startling lights and darks. An uncertain source of sunlight, bathing the scene from the upper left, skips across the heads and shoulders of the Apostles, landing on the torso and face of the dead woman. The bottom-heavy composition is balanced by a dramatically draped swag of red fabric in the top third of the image. Its folds are bathed in patterns of sunlight and deep shadow.

The nuns in the Church of Santa Maria della Scala in Rome's Trastevere neighborhood, who had commissioned the painting as their altarpiece, rejected it for its profane portrayal of the Virgin Mary. The scandalous painting subsequently had a long life as a commodity, first in Mantua, and subsequently in England, as it was bought and sold before becoming one of the treasures of the Louvre, going on display in 1793.

At 12 by 8 feet, this is a huge painting to pull from a wall—but as dramatic statements go, it's hard to imagine a more fitting farewell gesture for the signs-besotted Saunière.

THE LOUVRE'S LEONARDO PAINTINGS

Talk about a mother lode: the Louvre has more of Leonardo's major paintings than any other museum in the world. In fact, there are more of his major works here than in all of Italy. The outstanding collection was built up through royal acquisitions, starting with those of Leonardo's final patron, François I. Let's start with that legendary dame, the *Mona Lisa*.

Mona Lisa

When you enter the Salle des Etats, you may think you've stumbled across a red carpet appearance by Nicole Kidman or the Rolling Stones. Crowds pushing, cameras flashing, you may barely notice the 77 x 53 cm painting everyone is here to see: Leonardo's *Mona Lisa*, arguably the most famous painting in the Western world. Graceful under pressure, she stares out at us from a climate-controlled case, protected by bullet-proof, UV–resistant glass. A semicircular barrier keeps her admirers at arm's length.

When we look at the *Mona Lisa*, two questions immediately spring to mind. What's the big mystery? And is she worth the hype?

In the *Code*, Langdon summarizes some of the more offbeat theories about the *Mona Lisa*. The first—and least likely—of these theories is that the *Mona Lisa* is a portrait of Leonardo in drag. Many scholars, including heavyweights like Sigmund Freud, have speculated about Leonardo's homosexuality, and several drawings that may or may not be self-portraits of the artist bear some resemblance to the *Mona Lisa*. But there is no reason to make the leap to women's clothing. Leonardo searched for an ideal face—a representation of pure moral and physical beauty, an image beyond the usual boundaries of male and female—throughout his career. You will see reflections of this androgynous facial type in many of his works at the Louvre.

Of course, Langdon has his own theory about the *Mona Lisa*'s androgynous looks. He thinks she is not a real person at all, but a fusion of the ideal masculine and ideal feminine.

The winds of scholarship are always changing, but at this point, art historians are pretty much in agreement about the *Mona Lisa*'s identity. She was born Lisa Gherardini, in Florence in 1479. In 1495, at the age of 16, she married Francesco del Giocondo, the youngest son of a successful silk merchant. Already twice widowed, Giocondo was 19 years older than his bride, Monna (meaning "Madonna" or "Madame") Lisa. It is generally considered that the portrait, painted on poplar wood, was begun in Florence in 1503–4, but that Leonardo worked on it for several years, possibly as late as 1513–14.

Some scholars, including Oxford University's Martin Kemp, think the subject may have been pregnant when this portrait was painted. That would explain the taut, slightly swollen skin of her hands. Perhaps her famous smile expresses the satisfaction of one who, like the artist, was involved in an act of creation.

Her smile may also be a pun for her last name. Giocondo means "jovial" or "happy" in Italian—that's why the French call her *La Jaconde*, "the smiling one." Renaissance artists often included visual puns in their paintings as a kind of in-joke for the patron. Giorgio Vasari, a 15th-century commentator who wrote fly-on-the-wall accounts of the lives of Renaissance artists, tells yet another version of the story. He wrote that Leonardo kept the model busy with jesters and musicians.

The *Mona Lisa* became an international celebrity on August 21, 1911, when she was stolen from the Louvre. Vincenzo Perugia, a former Louvre employee and an Italian national, thought she should move back home to Florence. When the theft was discovered, newspapers and popular songs begged for her safe return. Crowds lined up to see the empty space on the wall. There was even an investigation into a *complot cubiste* (cubist conspiracy) which accused Picasso and the poet Apollinaire of stealing the painting to further the cause of modern art. The painting was found two years later in a hotel room in Florence, sewn into the lining of a traveling trunk, when Perugia tried to sell her to an Italian art dealer.

The *Mona Lisa*'s sojourn in Italy was not the end of her troubles. In 1956, the lower portion of the painting was severely damaged by an acid attack. That was the beginning of steadily increasing security measures.

All of these facts and figures don't seem to add up to the mysterious draw of the *Mona Lisa*. What is the X-factor that keeps people lining up to see her? **Vasari wrote about the *Mona Lisa* that "Anyone who looked very attentively at the hollow of her throat would see her pulse beating."** Perhaps we spend so much time with the *Mona Lisa* simply because she seems so *alive*. She stares right at us, challenging us to respond to her smile. The level of psychological realism here was totally new in the history of portraiture. We get a glimpse of her inner life. Instead of a static representation, Leonardo caught her in the act of thinking.

There is another less famous, but equally mysterious lady by Leonardo in the Louvre: his portrait of *La Belle Ferronnière*. Painted in the late 1490s, her gaze is as elusive as the *Mona Lisa*'s is direct. Try as we may, we can never quite meet her eyes. She is thought to be Lucrezia Crivelli, mistress of Ludovico Sforza, Leonardo's patron in Milan. The portrait's name comes from the little jewel she wears on her forehead, a fashion among court ladies of the period.

The Madonna of the Rocks

When Langdon and cryptographer Sophie Neveu run in to see the *Mona Lisa*, they find a clue written in black-light pen on the protective glass. They're then led to Leonardo's controversial *The Madonna of the Rocks*.

Leonardo was commissioned to paint *The Madonna of the Rocks* for the Confraternity of the Immaculate Conception in Milan in 1483. The cross-shaped composition shows the baby John the Baptist (on the left) praying to Jesus, the Virgin Mary (in the center) stretching her hand outward in a gesture of blessing, the Archangel Uriel (on the right) pointing to John the Baptist, and closest to the viewer, the baby Jesus looking up (perhaps toward God the Father) and making a gesture that looks a lot like a peace symbol.

Langdon thinks the Virgin Mary's "talony" hand is held out in a threatening gesture, possibly holding an invisible severed head that prefigures the fate of John the Baptist. But there is no art historical evidence to support such an interpretation. One of the reasons the hand seems to move so aggressively towards us in space is because of a technique called foreshortening. Foreshortening is a trick of perspective that makes an object look like it is poking out of the painting. Leonardo probably uses it here to make the hand look like it has crossed the imaginary space between the Virgin Mary in the background and where the baby Jesus is sitting in the foreground of the painting.

The painting may have sparked controversy because of the way Leonardo handled the iconography, or traditional symbolism, in the painting. He didn't give the figures halos to show their divinity, and he left out John the Baptist's cross, which would normally identify him.

Langdon thinks Leonardo went further and actually switched the babies, so that John is blessing Jesus, but there is no hard evidence to support such a radical interpretation. There is another version of this painting in the National Gallery in London (probably painted mostly by Leonardo's assistants), which shows a cross propped on John's shoulder and fills in the halos. In this less ambiguous rendition, John is on the left, being blessed. What we *do* know for sure about the painting is that there was a court battle over money. Leonardo and his assistants didn't think they were paid enough; their 800 lire advance barely covered the price of materials.

Despite potentially subversive undertones, the painting was a huge popular success. **Leonardo took care to make a connection with the viewer—see how the Archangel Uriel looks out to draw the viewer into the action of the painting.** The background, too, inspired admiration. Leonardo was a keen amateur botanist and geologist; his studies of plants, fossils, and rock formations guided his depiction of the grotto.

The Madonna of the Rocks is also an excellent example of Leonardo's unique way of painting, a technique called *sfumato* (*see* the sidebar *below*). It refers to the hazy atmosphere and soft shadows often seen in Leonardo's work. Instead of hard outlines, there is a gradual transition between light and shade, the impression that objects are dissolving in mist. It is sometimes difficult to tell where one object begins and another ends. These mysterious shadows are very much in contrast to the bright colors and linear outlines used by Leonardo's contemporaries such as Michelangelo and Raphael.

The Louvre has another excellent example of Leonardo's sfumato technique in his *Holy Family* or *The Virgin and Child with Saint Anne* (c. 1508–13). This painting shows three generations of

Sfumato

*L*eonardo's artwork embodies the paradox that less is more. He captured the complexity of the human face and figure in his art not by assiduously drawing every line and detail, but by blurring sections of his compositions, letting the viewer's imagination fill in the blanks. The technique is called *sfumato*, to make something looked "smoked." The most perfect examples of sfumato in Leonardo's work can be seen in the face of the angel in *The Madonna of the Rocks,* the heavily shadowed semblances in *The Virgin and Child with St. Anne,* and in the *Mona Lisa,* around the eyes and mouth. To achieve the effect, Leonardo smudged sharp

lines of paint or charcoal using his finger or a rag, creating gradations of value. Whether or not Leonardo invented sfumato is not known, but he used it so expertly and extensively in his art that the practice has become synonymous with his name.

Detail from Rocks.

the holy family: Saint Anne (mother of the Virgin Mary), the Virgin Mary, and the baby Jesus playing with a lamb. Notice how the subtle contours on the Virgin Mary's cheek and neck are defined solely by delicate shading. It gives the impression that we could reach out and touch, even dent, the flesh. This is one of Leonardo's unfinished paintings; you can see that the drapery on the Virgin Mary's blue cloak does not have the fine folds painted on the green sleeve.

Two *John the Baptist*s

There are two paintings of John the Baptist by Leonardo in the Louvre's collection. One, painted in Florence between 1513 and 1516, shows the smiling saint pointing to the cross, his skin luminous against a dark background. Most images of St. John the Baptist show us a baby or an emaciated old man, the prophet who foretells Christ's coming. Leonardo, however, depicted St. John as a vigorous young man, more like a mischievous pagan god than a devout Christian saint. The face is very androgynous, with soft contours, smooth, beardless skin, and an enigmatic smile—all part of Leonardo's continuing search for ideal beauty.

During the Renaissance, St. John the Baptist was a popular figure among philosophers trying to reconcile classical and Christian traditions. For some, St. John represented a new Adam; his androgynous traits recalled man before the creation of woman, before the separation of the sexes, and before original sin. For others, the androgyny recalled the myth of the hermaphrodite, man and woman made one by the gods.

Leonardo's second painting of St. John makes the pagan references even more explicit. Usually dated between 1510 and 1515, the painting appears to have been significantly reworked, probably after the artist's death. It shows a young man in a panther skin, holding a staff. This full-length painting of St. John looks like even more of a gender-bender than the first. The muscular chest and arms clearly contrast with the delicate, smooth features of the face. The current title of the painting, *Bacchus (Saint John the Baptist in the Desert)*, poses a difficult question: how can this painting be both Bacchus, the Greek god of wine, and St. John the Baptist? One hypothesis is that this started out as St. John the Baptist, holding his traditional wooden cross, and at some later date was altered to transform the cross into a *thyrsus*, the staff carried by Bacchus. Whatever the original composition, it is clear that Leonardo was playing with the similarities between Bacchus and St. John. Both wear panther skins as part of their traditional iconography, and both represent man's close association with nature, an idea that Leonardo investigated throughout his career.

The Chase Is On

HAVING FOUND MORE CLUES and a hidden key, Sophie and Langdon escape from the museum in Sophie's car. Meanwhile, a single-minded monk, Silas, has paid a visit to the church of St-Sulpice. St-Sulpice is known for the intriguing brass line that slices across the floor of the church—part of a sort of sundial.

THE CHAMPS-ELYSÉES

Named after the Greek Elysian Fields, the most famous street in France really *was* once fields on the outskirts of the Paris city limits. In 1616, Marie de' Medici had a long, tree-flanked pathway built here, so she could promenade up and down. A few decades later, Le Nôtre included this path in his plans for the Tuileries Gardens. Ever since then, the Champs has been the place to see and be seen in the City of Lights. Langdon and Sophie race along it as they try to reach the American Embassy.

The pathway gradually grew into a thoroughly modern boulevard, becoming part of Paris in 1828. To celebrate its new acquisition, the city installed footpaths, fountains, and gas lighting. Traces of this green past can be found at the end near place de la Concorde. Here the avenue begins with formal gardens and elegant Belle Epoque pavilions, which are now the historic restaurants Ledoyen, Laurent, and Le Pavillon Elysées. On a warm day, these gardens make a lovely, lilac-scented place to pause before tackling the Champs. Also at this end of the Champs stand the

As he moved toward the mist of the fountains, Langdon had the uneasy sense he was crossing an imaginary threshold into another world."
—*The Da Vinci Code*

The sprawling Louvre (above) has been a fortress, prison, palace, and museum. Over the centuries, it has weathered multiple renovations (far left), not to mention political upheaval, including the French Revolution and the 1830 uprising (left). By the 19th century, many of its galleries had become public art exhibition spaces (right).

A new entrance to the Louvre was built in the 1980s (top left). Modernist architect I.M. Pei (top center) unleashed a storm of controversy with his giant glass pyramid capping a subterranean entrance hall (top right).

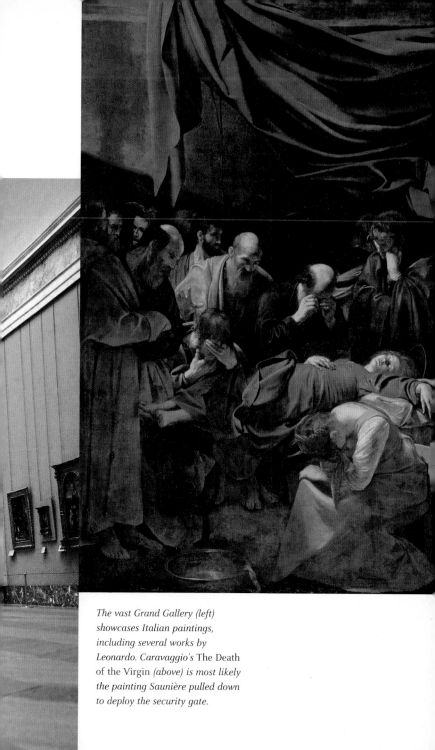

The vast Grand Gallery (left) showcases Italian paintings, including several works by Leonardo. Caravaggio's The Death of the Virgin *(above) is most likely the painting Saunière pulled down to deploy the security gate.*

An agent from the DCPJ (or PJ for short) interrupts Langdon's night at the Ritz Paris (above). This landmark hotel was the first to carry the Ritz name; it set a new high-water mark for luxury (right).

One of the world's most mesmerizing artworks is undoubtedly the Mona Lisa (below and right). The Italian nationalist who stole her in 1911 (left) claimed to have been bewitched by her beauty.

In his first version of the Madonna of the Rocks *(left), Leonardo painted a shadowy, mysterious setting—a bold and original move. A soft glow highlights the faces and gestures of the holy figures, infusing them with spiritual significance. Leonardo didn't follow the plan specified in his contract for this painting; rather than the prophets and troop of angels his clients had asked for, he introduced John the Baptist and included only one angel.*

In the second version of the Madonna of the Rocks *(right), Leonardo maintained his composition and craggy landscape but had to insert traditional halos and St. John's identifying cross to satisfy his clients' doctrinal requirements. The light is sharper, the forms firmer. The angel no longer looks out toward the viewer but casts his eyes down in reverie, and he no longer points a finger towards St. John.*

The Tuileries Gardens,
extending from the
Louvre, are the perfect
place to recover from
museum fatigue or
"Stendhal's syndrome"
(being overcome by
exquisite art).

Langdon passes the Arc du Carrousel on his way in and out of the Louvre.

Grand Palais and the Petit Palais, two lovely leftovers from the world's fair of 1900. Each of these domed, Belle Epoque structures, which originally served as exposition spaces, recently spent several years under renovation. In October 2005, the Grand Palais reopened with a splash, as crowds swarmed an art exhibit on turn-of-the-20th-century Viennese artists. The Petit Palais will soon follow suit and will display French painting and furniture.

The Champs is a favorite parade ground for Bastille Day and other extravaganzas. It's also the finish line for the Tour de France, where American cyclist and cancer survivor Lance Armstrong celebrated his seventh consecutive Tour win in July 2005. After a slump into tackiness in the 1980s, the Champs has regained its reputation as an elegant place for a stroll and a bit of window-shopping. At the turn of this millennium, the city overhauled the street, installing wider sidewalks and polished street furniture. Stores such as Sephora (the cosmetics giant), Guerlain (the perfume house), and the Drugstore Publicis (pharmacy meets shiny arcade) all make the Champs a popular place to visit, especially since many shops stay open late.

There are also movie theaters and hip nightclubs, but the most surprising trendy element on the Champs is its car dealerships. Not your standard car lot, the Atelier Renault (at No. 53) claims some of the most interesting new interior design and architecture in the city—it's well worth checking out. Though somewhat overpriced, the avenue's cafés are great for people-watching even late into the night, when the lights shine on the Champs' crowning glory, the Arc de Triomphe.

Inspired by Rome's Arch of Titus, the colossal Arc de Triomphe was supposed to celebrate Napoleon's military successes. But its sculpture-covered walls weren't completed on schedule, and when the Emperor married Marie-Louise (after ingloriously dumping Josephine), the Arc had to be faked with a painted canvas. The monument was finally completed in 1836, long after Napoleon's fall from glory. Today, if you don't suffer from vertigo, you can climb up to the top of the Arc for an impressive view of Paris. If you'd rather stay on the ground, be sure to check out the magnificent relief sculpture by François Rude—especially his *The Departure of the Volunteers of 1792*. Better known as *La Marseillaise*, this tautly expressive work is on the right side of the arch when standing on the Champs-Elysées. France's Unknown Soldier is buried beneath the Arc; the flame is rekindled every evening at 6:30 p.m.

In the *Code*, the Arc de Triomphe appears briefly when Sophie guns her SmartCar around the Etoile, the death-defying traffic circle that surrounds the arch. A few years ago, the media had a field day when the French Minister of Transport had a minor car accident here. To emerge unharmed from this insane roundabout is considered the essential rite of passage for Parisian drivers; rumor has it that someone had intentionally targeted the minister's car as he drove around. In the novel, Sophie is speeding away from the American Embassy when she whips towards the roundabout. Luckily, there wouldn't be too many other cars swirling around the Etoile at 2:51 a.m.

GARE ST-LAZARE

Brown describes Gare St-Lazare as "the awkward offspring of an airplane hangar and a greenhouse." True, it's a bit shabby, but in the right light, this train station is awfully romantic. Journal-writer Anaïs Nin used to wait here for novelist Henry Miller during their torrid affair in the 1930s. It's the oldest railway station in Paris, with a posh façade from 1889 stuck on top of an old glass-and-iron train shed from the 1840s. Groggy British backpackers disembark here, coming in from the Channel ferries and from Normandy. Sophie uses this station to leave a false trail for the police, buying tickets to Lille on Langdon's credit card. Nowadays, trains for Lille leave from the grander Gare du Nord; St-Lazare is mostly used by commuters, heading home to the 'burbs.

In the plaza outside, there are two sculptures by contemporary French artist Arman. But art-lovers particularly seek out this station because of its importance to the Impressionists. In 1874, Edouard Manet first showed *Le Chemin de Fer* ("The Railway") at the Paris Salon. This painting, often called *Gare Saint-Lazare*, shows a small girl watching trains through an iron fence, beside a seated woman with a dog. The work was condemned because it depicted an urban, almost industrial scene. But this is exactly what interested Manet: trains represented a new era, something flawed but exciting. Manet's painting studio was next door to this station; walk uphill around the tracks to see the views he painted.

He wasn't alone in his fascination. Fellow artists Gustave Caillebotte and Claude Monet also painted here, inspired by the way the station's glass roof refracted light through the steam of arriving trains. The train station also provided the painters with a handy escape route into the Normandy countryside. To see some of their paintings while you're in Paris, visit the Impressionist and Postimpressionist museum, the Musée d'Orsay—as a former train station, the Orsay would surely impress Manet! ⊠ *Rue St-Lazare and rue d'Amsterdam, 8ᵉ arrondissement.* Ⓜ *St-Lazare.*

THE BAWDY BOIS DE BOULOGNE

The Bois de Boulogne is an intriguing mix of aristocratic provenance and grit. It became a public park during the sparkling Second Empire of the mid-1800s. The sheer size of the Bois, along with its innumerable shady pathways, makes it an ideal place for the illicit nighttime action seen by a squeamish Langdon during his aborted taxi ride with Sophie.

Brown points out that Parisians call the Bois de Boulogne the "Garden of Earthly Delights," a reference to the freak-filled painting by Hieronymus Bosch. Bosch's work in the Louvre should give you an idea of the nightly atmosphere in the Bois, as prostitutes prowl for clients. Even in daylight, the park's most secluded paths should be avoided by women walking alone.

This 2,200-acre park was wilderness until Napoleon III entrusted the Bois to his chief renovator, Baron Haussmann. The Baron and his brilliant friend and landscaper, Alphand, redesigned the woods into a London-style park. On sunny days, join the pilgrimage from the city into the prettily landscaped Pré Catalan and Bagatelle gardens (follow signs to find them). Or you could stroll around the photogenic Lac Inférieur, which is easily reached on foot from the métro. You can also rent a rowboat on either of the park's two lakes. Be sure to check the papers if you're a horse enthusiast—meetings at the Longchamp and

Auteuil racetracks offer Parisians a chance to dress up and bet wildly.

The French Open tennis tournament at the Roland Garros stadium in late May is another swell occasion. It's towards this stadium that Sophie drives to find the fictional Depository Bank of Zurich. A note about the Porte Dauphine métro station at the park's entrance: The station has one of the few Art Nouveau iron-and-glass entrances designed by Hector Guimard that's still in its original location. ⊠ *Main entrance at bottom of av. Foch.* Ⓜ *Porte Dauphine, Porte Maillot, or Porte d'Auteuil.*

A DEAD END AT ST-SULPICE

Langdon and Sophie aren't the only ones on an urgent mission. An Opus Dei monk, Silas, believes he'll find a crucial clue from the Priory of Sion, a secret society, hidden in one of Paris's Left Bank churches, the Eglise St-Sulpice. Imposing and tomb-like, St-Sulpice hovers over its square like a stern disciplinarian. Its formidable presence is in striking contrast to the rest of the neighborhood, where pleasure is a way of life.

By day the tree-lined plaza bustles with pigeons and sidewalk musicians, while the Fountain of the Four Bishops splashes at its center. Elegant boutiques, such as Yves Saint-Laurent and Christian Lacroix, make the surrounding streets some of the city's most fashionable, and chic Parisians mingle with tourists at the popular Café de la Mairie, whose street-side tables face St-Sulpice's façade.

By night, however, this wealthy neighborhood shuts down tight. Few would notice a Silas pounding on the door at 1 a.m. But even without a murderous monk prowling about, the hulking church, lit by floodlights that emphasize its unfinished towers and severe, double-colonnaded portico, appears menacing.

While there's no hard evidence to suggest that a temple to Isis ever existed here, place St-Sulpice does have ancient roots. The church was created, so it is thought, in the seventh or eighth century, as a satellite to nearby St-Germain-des-Prés. Once a rural backwater outside the city, the St-Sulpice parish slowly developed into an urban neighborhood of grand aristocratic residences. In

1120, a new sanctuary was built and dedicated to St. Sulpice (570–647), who served several Merovingian kings and was also royal chaplain to the Merovingian ruler Clotaire II. (The Merovingian dynasty, perhaps not incidentally, is the line that Teabing claims descends from Jesus Christ.)

In 1646, Anne d'Autriche, regent for her young son Louis XIV, laid the first stone of a much larger, grander church. There were many cooks in the architectural kitchen, including Louis Le Vau and Daniel Gittard, and the design changed many times during construction. When money ran out in 1678, work came to a grinding halt.

> **L E O   S A Y S**
>
> "Why does the eye see a thing more clearly in dreams than the imagination when awake?"

Not much happened construction-wise until the arrival 40 years later of a new curate, Jean-Baptiste Languet de Gergy. He lit a fire under the building process, but it wasn't until 1732 that Giovanni Servandoni won the architectural competition for the façade. His design scheme employed a classical theme inspired by ancient Rome. Four years later, Gilles-Marie Oppenordt, a student of Mansart, completed the nave, and the church, though still unfinished, was consecrated on June 30, 1745. Around this time, work also began on the brass line that Silas sought (*see* Walk the Line, *below*).

Although Servandoni's structure was a bold statement of his time—neoclassicism was all the rage—the cavernous interior is a rich mix of styles and influences. The frescoed ceiling by François Lemoyne, glorifying the Madonna's ascent into heaven, harks back to the baroque while the wide, arched windows are a nod to Enlightenment clarity.

Rose windows and carved rosettes lighten the somber setting, originally planned to draw the eye to Edme Bouchardon's six-foot silver statue of the Virgin and Child inside the Virgin's Chapel behind the choir. (Rumor has it that Languet stole the necessary silver from his dinner hosts.) The statue proved a challenge to guard from thieves, so it was replaced in 1744 by Jean-Baptiste Pigalle's frothy white-marble version, which is still there.

In the transept windows you can spot the letters *P* and *S*—but these initials designate "Pierre" (Peter) and "Sulpice," not Priory of Sion or Princesse Sophie.

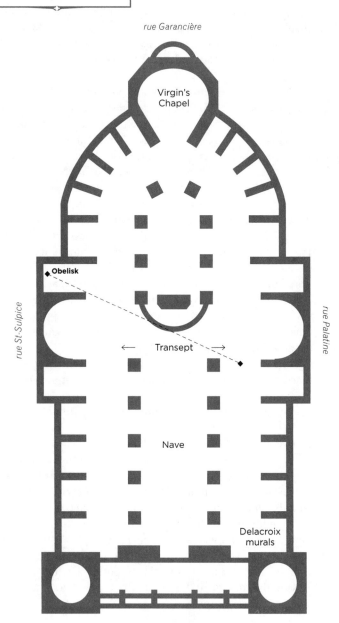

ST-SULPICE

rue Garancière

Virgin's Chapel

Obelisk

rue St-Sulpice

rue Palatine

← Transept →

Nave

Delacroix murals

Place St-Sulpice

A Temple for All Causes

St-Sulpice seemed cursed by natural disasters and accidents. Too heavy to support itself, Oppenordt's campanile had to be demolished. In 1762, a fire damaged the church, and in 1770 lightning bolts destroyed the façade's pediment. Ouch.

A few years later, Jean-François Chalgrin replaced the pediment with a balustrade and strangely asymmetrical towers, one square, one octagonal. The French Revolution and its turbulent aftermath then halted construction and catapulted St-Sulpice into most unorthodox practices.

In 1793, the state confiscated all church property (a move initiated by St-Sulpice seminary's most infamous graduate, diplomat Charles-Maurice de Talleyrand-Périgord). St-Sulpice was renamed the Temple of Reason. (For its consecration, an actress played the goddess Reason.) Wooden statues of St. Peter and St. Sulpice were removed from their niches and burned.

During the subsequent Reign of Terror, the church became the Temple of the Supreme Being, and when the next regime invented the pantheistic cult of Théophilanthropie (what a mouthful), St-Sulpice was consecrated the Temple of Victory. There, Paris feted General Napoleon Bonaparte's return from Egypt in 1799 with a banquet for 750 guests. Three days later, he staged his historic coup d'état.

Napoleon reestablished Catholicism in France, and as a result, St-Sulpice was refurbished, although its façade remains hauntingly unfinished. Notable 19th-century additions include action-packed, though darkened, paintings for the Chapel of the Holy Angels by the Romantic master, Eugène Delacroix (Talleyrand's unacknowledged bastard) and Aristide Cavaillé-Coll's 100-stop organ, which is still often used for concerts and services today. ⊠ *Pl. St-Sulpice, 6ᵉ arrondissement. 01–46–33–21–78.* Ⓜ *St-Sulpice.*

WALK THE LINE

St-Sulpice's obelisk, or gnomon, stands like a giant, white marble metronome whose pendulum rod has been fixed permanently into place. As Silas was told by his Teacher, the gnomon

The Prime Line at Greenwich Observatory

t-Sulpice and the Rose Line in Paris may be grabbing attention these days, but let's not forget that Greenwich, England has been home to the Prime Meridian for over a century.

A meridian is an arbitrary north-south line used as a reference point. Using a standard meridian is essential for nautical navigation; people have calculated them at least since the 2nd century A.D. As global sea trade and the number of floundering sailors escalated, so did the need for an official navigation line. In 1884, delegates from 25 nations met in Washington, D.C., to designate a standard meridian and set a universal time.

Greenwich won almost unanimously, which is no surprise given that Britain was then the most powerful country in the world. The French lobbied unsuccessfully for the meridian they'd charted through Paris and the establishment of Paris Mean Time.

The Royal Observatory at Greenwich is an easy day trip from London. There you can straddle the brass Prime line—one foot in the Eastern Hemisphere, one in the West. ⊠ *Greenwich Park, Greenwich, 020–8312–6565, www.rog.nmm.ac.uk.*

works as the vertical portion of a giant sundial mapped out on the church's floor.

The obelisk is set against the wall of the northernmost point of the church's Latin-cross interior. A thin, gilded line runs from the golden ball and cross at its top, down the center of its obelisk-shaped shaft, and bisects the official engravings at its base. Bending horizontally, a narrow brass stripe, no more than a quarter of an inch wide, continues on an exact north-south axis along the floor. Time has worn the metal strip into the gray marble surrounding it, making it difficult to spot—but once you've seen it, it's hard to look at anything else. On a visit, you should be able to walk along part of it, but do keep in mind that this is a working church with services and other activities.

Cutting across the transept, the line rises up three low marble steps to the choir and heads to a spot in front of the center of the altar. There, it reaches a brass oval, set into the gray-and-white tiled floor behind the balustrade, before descending the far side of the stairs. It continues south of the crossing to a rectangular marble plaque in the floor and suddenly halts.

At exactly noon, according to old Paris time (nine minutes and twenty-one seconds ahead of Greenwich time), light passing through a small aperture high above the south transept marks a spot along this line. On December 21, the winter solstice, sunlight hits the obelisk; on June 21, summer solstice, the floor plaque; and at the spring and autumn equinoxes, the oval in the choir.

Marrying science and faith, Languet de Gergy, curate of St-Sulpice, commissioned the "ecclesiastical compass" in the 1720s to determine the exact date of Easter, which, according to the Gregorian calendar, should be celebrated near the first full moon after the spring equinox. English astronomer and clock maker Henry Sully began construction on this Enlightenment sundial, inspired partially by a description of one in the 1st century B.C. by Vitruvius (whose ideas also lay behind Leonardo's *Vitruvian Man*). After Sully's death, Pierre-Charles Lemonnier of the Academie des Sciences took over. Claude Langlois, an academician, who also worked as an engineer at the Louvre, finished it in 1744.

Their efforts paid off. Astonishingly, daily measurements from the gnomon allowed astronomers from the Paris Observatory to calculate that the pivoting of the earth's axis diminishes 45 seconds every century, a rotation never previously understood. Contemporary estimates amend this rate to 46.85 seconds; this nearly perfect result testifies to the gnomon's accuracy.

However, St-Sulpice's line does not quite mesh with the official Paris Meridian Line (now longitude 2°20' east). The Paris Meridian Line, called the Rose Line in the *Code*, is measured from the nearby Paris Observatory. On Midsummer's Day in 1667, members of the Royal Academy ceremonially broke ground on the observatory, whose site was calculated to exactly bisect the north-south zero meridian plotted by French astronomer Jean Picard in 1655. Although an international conference in 1884 placed 0° longitude in Greenwich, England (*see* the Greenwich sidebar, *above*), the French kept using their own prime meridian until the early 20th century. Even after the world had officially adopted Greenwich Mean Time, the French referred to it by the unwieldy and rather ludicrous name, "Paris Mean Time retarded by nine minutes twenty-one seconds."

TRACKING THE ROSE LINE
THROUGH THE PALAIS ROYAL

To find the Parisian Rose Line, follow Langdon's route and head into the Palais Royal. Here you'll see a series of small, round, bronze medallions set into the pavement. These "Arago disks" that stud the city are actually a relatively recent arrival. In 1984, the French held a competition to design a monument commemorating French astronomers. A Dutch artist named Jan Dibbets came up with a unique idea: instead of a traditional sculpture, he designed a path named for François Arago (1786–1853), the man who precisely calculated the Paris Meridian, or Rose Line. Each 5-inch disk is marked N/S (North/South) with the name Arago in the center. Dibbets's 135 disks trace the meridian from Sacré Coeur in Montmartre to the far side of the Luxembourg Gardens. The Louvre has three disks in the floor of the Denon Wing and five in the Cour Carrée, beyond the glass pyramid entrance. Seven disks parade through the Palais Royal.

Langdon starts his walk at the north end of the Palais Royal neighborhood, on rue des Petits-Champs. When he turns south down rue Richelieu, he walks past the brick-and-stone Bibliothèque Nationale Richelieu. This building used to be the French National Library, the one mentioned by Dan Brown in his preface. Named for the powerful 17th-century Cardinal Richelieu, the library contained more than 7 million volumes. (Most are now in the Bibliothèque Nationale François-Mitterand on the Left Bank.) Today, the Richelieu hosts temporary photography exhibitions, with everyone from Cartier-Bresson and Man Ray to contemporary photographers like Sophie Calle. Researchers still consult original manuscripts, coins, and prints here.

Farther down rue Richelieu, small arched passages lead to rue de Montpensier and into the Palais Royal's lovely gardens. Parts of the *palais* date from the 1630s, when all-powerful Cardinal Richelieu magnanimously bequeathed the building to Louis XIII. Louis XIV lived here as a child and here he conquered his first mistress, Louise de la Vallière.

Later, in 1780, Louis-Philippe d'Orléans, the king's cousin, had splendid passageways built, naming each wing after one of his sons: Montpensier, Beaujolais, and Valois. Gambling and prostitution flourished here, as the Duke refused to allow police inside the gates. During the French Revolution, the gardens became Le Palais Egalité ("the Palace of Equality") because Louis-Philippe professed revolutionary ideas—and even came up with a plan to convert the arcades of the palace into boutiques and cafés. Louis XVI reputedly quipped, "My cousin, now that you are going to keep shop, I suppose we shall see you only on Sundays." Today, Louis-Philippe's idea has come to fruition: the arcades include Didier Ludot's boutique devoted to vintage couture, the elegant perfume counter at Shiseido, and an entire shop devoted to deviously constructed mechanical children's toys.

One of the oldest restaurants in Paris is here, the Grand Véfour, with its original Directoire interior. Nearly every seat is marked with a plaque commemorating a famous patron, from Napoleon to Jean Cocteau. Farther along this Beaujolais wing, French writer Colette lived in a small apartment. The first woman to be awarded the French Légion d'Honneur, Colette moved here in 1927 with her third husband (a man 17 years younger than she) and spent most of the next 25 years writing by her Palais Royal window, sitting up in bed. It's easy to see why she liked the view: the neoclassical arcades surround lush flowerbeds, while the paths beneath the regimented trees echo with soccer-playing children. And there is usually at least one senior citizen crumbling croissants for the sparrows.

For many years, residents of the Palais Royal had an especially impressive timepiece: a small cannon. It was positioned on the Rose Line and at noon every day the miniature bronze gun went off. The cannon boomed the hour from 1786 to 1914 and again from 1975 to the early 1990s.

At the south end of the Palais Royal, a courtyard separates the Comédie Française (the famous theater company founded in 1680) and the Ministry of Culture. The space is filled with irregularly cropped, striped black-and-white columns. These were installed in 1986 by French artist Daniel Buren; initially, Parisians loved to hate these modern pillars. But Buren has gradually become more popular as an artist and these days the Palais Royal has black-and-white striped blinds to match its Buren columns. Exit the Palais Royal towards the Café de Nemours and you'll see the easiest-to-spot Arago disk. From here, Robert crossed rue de Rivoli. Kids on rollerblades and skates often practice their jumps here; you can dodge past them to the far side of rue de Rivoli, where the Louvre awaits.

CHÂTEAU VILLETTE: HIDEOUT FOR A (K)NIGHT

Château Villette, a relatively pocket-sized palace, is an ideal lair for the scheming Sir Leigh Teabing. The 185-acre estate would certainly appeal to his taste, his need for privacy—and his penchant for drama.

About 30 miles northwest of Paris, Château Villette mimics the grandiose sprawl of the palace of Versailles 22 miles south. But while Versailles is all gilded extravagance, Villette favors harmonious proportion and calmly rendered solitude.

It's no accident that Villette resembles Versailles—two of Louis XIV's favorite contractors crafted both châteaux. Jean Dyel II, Count of Aufflay, commissioned Villette in 1668, the year that Louis inaugurated the Versailles gardens. Architect François Mansart, one of the king's favorites and a Versailles veteran, began work on Villette. When Mansart died, his grand-nephew, Jules Hardouin-Mansart, who also worked on Versailles, finished Villette.

Dyel had a clear vision for Villette, tempering grandeur with order. He was the French ambassador to Venice, and his exposure to Venetian art and architecture may have predisposed him to Andrea Palladio's geometric villas. The result is a château with symmetrical wings of handsomely proportioned rooms, evenly placed glass-paned doors and windows, and a garden with carefully organized planes of lawns, hedges, and water.

The château's front doors lead into the stone entry, a rectangle with a pure oval tightly set within it. From here a staircase gently curls upwards at the right. You can look into the octagonal salon and, through its glass-paned doors, see the gardens beyond.

The château's grounds echo the work of France's most celebrated gardener, André Le Nôtre. Here you can see the essential qualities of a late-17th- and early-18th-century *jardin à la française,* in which logic reins in freewheeling nature. Classical sculptures and urns punctuate the linear geometry of lawns, hedges, and man-made ponds. Fountains spout gravity-defying jets of water and hidden pathways lead to statues of pagan deities. Striking views open up where least expected. A statue of the un-

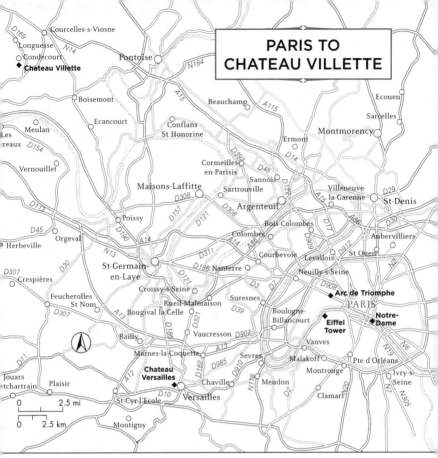

ruly water god Neptune sits atop a steep series of cascading fountains, while on the hill behind him stands an ancient obelisk.

The château also had its very own truth-seeking Sophie: Marie-Louis-Sophie, née de Grouchy, who was born at the château in 1764. Criticized for reading too much Enlightenment philosophy, for writing letters of distressing honesty, for her inappropriate closeness to General Lafayette and other, even more torrid affairs, this Sophie had a melodramatic life. With her lover as witness, she married the liberal philosopher and mathematician Marie-Jean-Antoine Nicolas de Caritat, Marquis de Condorcet, in Villette's chapel. Condorcet's free-thinking could not save his aristocratic neck during the French Revolution, so he committed suicide in prison before reaching the guillotine.

California realtor Olivia Hsu Decker bought Villette in 1999 and restored it to include 18 bedrooms, 21 bathrooms and various salons. While Decker modernized the château's phone system, she refrained from installing a high-tech intercom or state-of-the-art surveillance equipment. But happily, if you need to hide a cryptex in a hurry, there's a deep-cushioned divan in the wood-paneled library.

While the château is not generally open to the public, it does offer two-hour *Da Vinci Code* tours (€35–€95 per person). For a princely sum, you can spend the night or indulge in a five-night *Code* package, including meals and trips to sites covered in the novel. The château is also available for weddings (there's a private chapel on the grounds) and holds cooking classes and concerts. ⊠ *Chemin de la Maison Blanche, Condecourt 95450, France, 01–34–42–80–80, www.frenchvacation.com.*

history lessons

Curiouser & Curiouser

LANGDON AND SOPHIE FLEE to the estate of Langdon's friend Sir Leigh Teabing, a Grail expert. Over wee-hours tea, Teabing reveals that the Holy Grail isn't an object but a person, Mary Magdalene. Langdon and Teabing give Sophie a surprising version of early Christian history and explain how the Priory of Sion has long protected the devastating evidence of the Grail's true nature. A threatening visit by Silas spurs them all to board Teabing's plane for a late-night flight to London.

THE PRIORY OF SION'S MURKY HISTORY

Skull and Bones, the Fists of Righteous Harmony, the Loyal Order of Moose, the Odd Fellows—whatever you may think about secret societies, you've got to give them credit for having intriguing names.

The name of the Priory of Sion conjures up ideas of faith and long-established tradition. But while representatives of the Priory of Sion have claimed that their organization has kept its existence well-hidden for centuries, their secret society actually appears to have been an elaborate con game pulled off by a royal wannabe.

In the preface to the *Code*, Brown states that the Priory is a "real organization ... a European secret society founded in 1099" with an illustrious membership that included Botticelli, Sir Isaac Newton, and, of course, Leonardo. But in fact the Priory of Sion was founded in 1956 by a man named Pierre-Athanase-Marie Plantard. The organization was named after the hill of Mont Sion outside of Annemasse, in the south of France, where Plantard reportedly planned to build a spiritual retreat center.

Plantard gathered four founding members for the order: André Bonhomme (president), Jean Delaval (vice president), Pierre Plantard (secretary-general), and Armand Defago (treasurer). According to documents Plantard filed with Annemasse's bureau of records, the Priory had a fairly ho-hum agenda: to consolidate support for local politicians and to restore chivalry to the modern world. But in the mid-1960s Plantard began to boast about the league's deep occult roots and its role as the protector of the Merovingian lineage, a dynasty of Frankish kings who ruled parts of present-day France and Germany from the 5th to 8th century A.D. Plantard also said he was the last surviving member of the Merovingian family—a strange flight of fancy given that he was descended from a long line of decidedly less-than-glamorous laborers.

There is no definitive list of Priory of Sion members nor are there available records of meetings or activities. But Brown didn't come up with his membership lists out of thin air. Lists of all of the supposed Priory Grand Masters from the 12th century through the 20th were discovered stashed away in France's National Library in 1975. They were part of a small compilation of supposedly ancient documents collectively known as the "Dossiers Secrets," which were allegedly found by a librarian during a routine inventory check. The Dossiers also included genealogies of the Merovingian line (helpfully validating Plantard's claim to royal relations) and an account of the founding of the Priory of Sion in 1099 by Godefroy de Bouillon.

Few people outside of France knew anything of this discovery or the Priory of Sion before the 1982 publication of *Holy Blood, Holy Grail* by British journalists Michael Baigent, Richard Leigh, and Henry Lincoln. The Dossiers were a central source for the book, which puts forth the idea—now familiar to readers of the

Code—that Jesus was married, had children, and his bloodline, the Merovingian dynasty, was protected by the Priory of Sion and their well-armed buddies the Knights Templar.

But it turned out that the Dossiers were not what they seemed.

Plantard's associate Philippe de Chérisey later confessed that he helped forge the documents in 1965–1967, and that he helped plant them in the library during the same time period. Plantard eventually admitted the Dossiers were bogus, but claimed that the forgeries were created by copying original documents which he possessed (though these didn't materialize).

Plantard's claims became even wilder after *Holy Blood, Holy Grail* was published. He was rather brutally exposed as a fraud by French journalist Jean-Luc Chaumeil in 1984, but attempted to make a comeback in 1989. This time, he claimed that the Priory had been founded in 1681 at the mysterious French town of Rennes-le-Château (*see* Holy Hokum, *below*) and added a name to the infamous Grand Master list: Roger-Patrice Pelat, a well-known financier and friend of then-President of France François Mitterrand.

Bad move. Pelat had been involved in a huge insider stock-trading scandal and died (some claim he was murdered) before the investigation was concluded. In 1993 Plantard was asked to provide evidence to the court on Pelat's background. Judge Thierry Jean-Pierre, perturbed by Plantard's testimony, ordered a search of Plantard's home and then required Plantard to swear on oath that his Priory of Sion tales concerning Pelat were true. Plantard admitted he'd lied, and was sternly warned not to toy with the French courts.

Plantard vanished from public life after that incident and died on February 3, 2000 in Paris. Two authors of *Holy Blood, Holy Grail* have since stated in interviews that they now believe the tales Plantard told them about the Priory of Sion were not firmly rooted in truth.

Still, references to the Priory of Sion pop up somewhat regularly in popular culture, presented as a serious secret society or a joke. There is even a band named "Priory of Brion," formed by Led Zeppelin's Robert Plant in 1999. The name winks at both the Priory and the Monty Python film *Life of Brian*. According to Plant's Web site, though, you shouldn't hold your breath for an album.

Holy Hokum

Visitors to the ancient church of Ste-Marie Madeleine at Rennes-le-Château, in the Languedoc region of southern France, are greeted with a carving that reads *Terribilis Est Locus Iste* or "This Place is Terrible." It's not exactly the average church welcome mat.

Inside the tiny stone church, a statue of the demon Asmodeus balances a holy water font on his back, and there are unusual takes on the iconography of the Stations of the Cross. The odd decoration has convinced some that the church is one big encoded message.

The curious decor is the work of Bérenger Saunière (that last name sounds familiar, no?), who began serving as village priest of Rennes-le-Château in 1885. In 1891, the previously impoverished priest suddenly began buying land and redecorating the 11th-century church.

No one knows for sure how Saunière managed to fund his projects. When his exuberant building binge began, so did the gossip. Some believed the priest had unearthed the fabled treasure of the Templars, items taken from Solomon's Temple, which many locals believe was hidden in the area.

Church records from the time indicate that Saunière was "trafficking in masses," or advertising his willingness to say masses for departed and nearly departed souls for sizable fees. A church investigation revealed that Saunière collected the money but never performed the masses. As punishment, he was forbidden to say masses until he returned the money to its rightful owners, which he was unable to do.

Saunière denied the charges and took the secret of his financial windfall to his grave in 1917. His housekeeper was the beneficiary of his will, and she eventually sold all the property to local restaurateur Noel Corbu, who decided that the best way to draw tourists to the out-of-the-way town was to play up the mysterious church.

In the mid-1950s, Corbu met Pierre Plantard. Soon after their meeting, a story began to circulate that the treasure Saunière discovered was actually a cache of ancient documents belonging to the Priory of Sion. These documents supposedly told of the survival of Jesus' descendants and were so potentially explosive that

Saunière was paid by the Catholic Church to keep them under wraps. The story became the focus of several popular books, among them *Holy Blood, Holy Grail.*

Corbu was right about one thing: the fantastic church and the equally fantastic tale launched a lively tourist trade, which has only increased since the publication of *The Da Vinci Code.* For further information and photos of the church, see www.rennes-discovery.com.

CONSTANTINE: SMOOTH OPERATOR

In *The Da Vinci Code,* Teabing clearly relished making Sophie's head spin with the tale of how a Roman emperor with a weakness for sun worship turned his vast pagan empire to Christianity. According to the crafty knight, it was Constantine who "shaped the face of Christianity as we know it today." But how did Constantine get to exercise such awesome power? The same way he came to unite and rule a long-fractured empire. Constantine had prodigious military skills, a Clintonesque knack for political triangulation, a Roman emperor's gift for assassination, and, possibly, a bit of spiritual curiosity.

By the time Constantine began his bloody campaign to rule the Roman Empire in 305, Christianity had attracted enough followers to seriously bedevil the officially pagan Roman state. Even centuries after crucifying Jesus, the state refused to accept Christianity. And the pagans—the majority of Romans at the time—violently opposed Christians' refusal to properly worship their various and sundry gods. To the pagans, Christians provoked these deities to avenge themselves via natural disasters and other misfortunes. Yet Christianity was such a disunified faith that one of the few things its adherents shared was their persecuted status. In 303, the Emperor Diocletian launched the Great Persecution to finish off the tenacious movement once and for all. *Great* was no exaggeration. Officials tried to systematically purge the entire Roman Empire of Christians. Instead, they simply provided the faithful with more martyrs to extol.

The turmoil was not limited to the religious arena. Following Diocletian's abdication in 305, a power vacuum left the empire in chaos. The East and West were split, with some half dozen would-be successors vying for control. Enter the ambitious general Constantine. The son of a powerful general, Constantine's success was more than mere nepotism. **A crack military leader in his own right, Constantine saw the Latin on the wall. Or, rather, in the sky.**

Just before a decisive battle to control the western empire, Constantine had a vision. After seeing a cross-shaped symbol in the sky along with the message *In hoc signo vinces* ("in this sign, conquer"), Constantine saw the light: if he would put his faith in the Christian God, he would triumph. Triumph he did. Charging under the sign of the cross, the pagan general won the West and found the Christian God to be a useful ally. And in 312, despite his apparent continuation of certain pagan practices such as sun worship, he officially converted to Christianity. The following year Constantine issued the Edict of Milan, which ended the persecution of Christians. Constantine spread the good word, convincing his lone remaining rival Licinius, who ruled the East, to agree to the détente as well.

What Price Solidarity?

Constantine had savvily appraised the zeitgeist. His support of Christianity became lavish and, as Teabing says, meddlesome. It seems that Constantine's most pressing interest in church doctrine was not personal salvation, but in getting everyone on the same page. One god was an improvement over the multitude of regional pagan deities, but he wanted more. He wanted to unify his fractured empire under Christianity, and he needed the factions of the church to stop squabbling like, well, Christians and pagans. But with no obvious winner, he threw his support to different factions over the years in hopes of solidifying the church and its ever-growing ranks of adherents.

Still, Constantine probably relied more on steely-eyed strategy than divine intervention in favoring the branches of Christianity that emphasized the Old Testament. Following in the footsteps of the kings of Israel, Constantine further increased his power base using the good book's example of entwining the imperial and the religious. Many bishops, who had become used to a life of banishment and hardship, came to appreciate this newfound attention and empowerment by the state. The generous taxpayer funding of projects, such as manufacturing 50 copies of the Bible in Latin (by hand, of course), and new church construction, spread the faith and helped ease any misgivings church officials may have felt.

Finally in 324, after years of uneasy coexistence, Constantine defeated Licinius in the East and laid unrivalled claim to the entire Roman Empire. How to unify his hard-won subjects? Quickly, he decided something must be done about the increasingly contentious disputes of belief within the church. The following year, he brought together the first ecumenical council, the Council of Nicea. Composed of 230 church leaders, the Council had many orders of business to iron out. But its most critical job was to resolve a debate raging in Alexandria over the nature of Christ's divinity.

While explaining his theory on how Christianity evolved, Teabing tells Sophie that in the early days of Christianity, Jesus was considered "a mortal prophet . . . a great and powerful man, but a *man* nonetheless." Most scholars believe that early Christians considered Christ to be, in some sense, divine. Many theories tried to clarify how Jesus could be human yet divine, to say nothing of how the Son of God plus God equaled one deity. But no theory was the final word—the issue was an ongoing debate. By the early 320s an Alexandrian preacher named Arius was gaining a wide following. He taught that while Jesus was indeed divine, he was also God's first creation—like God, but not the same.

To a young deacon named Athanasius and many other officials, this was the top of a slippery slope that ended with Christ losing his status as Lord and Savior. They countered that Christ had always existed, was fully divine, and was of the same essence as God. To 21st-century ears the debate sounds like a matter of semantics, and, indeed, in Greek the two positions worked out to a difference of an *I*: *homiousios*, "of similar substance," versus *homoousios*, "the same substance." But the disagreement was divisive and had to be resolved. In the end, a majority of the bishops agreed with Athanasius and drafted the Nicene Creed, spelling out the Trinity. The Creed stated that the three parts of the Trinity, the Father, the Son, and the Holy Ghost, are all of one substance, and all part of one God.

Despite Teabing's view, it's unlikely that Constantine had anything to do with the Council's outcome—he just wanted a verdict to lay down the law. He was more than willing to throw his authority around for the victor, but not particularly vested in who it would be. Even after the Council, Constantine continued to shift his support among church officials in hopes of keeping the peace. Teabing is right on the money in questioning Constantine's credentials as a Christian, however. But in the end, the upshot mattered much more than Constantine's own fondness for the sun god. He had stopped the inevitable clash of empire and Christianity and started a symbiotic relationship that just about conquered the world. Constantine had forged an empire with one religion, one god, one emperor.

LOST EPISODES OF THE APOSTLES

Teabing's taste for villainy trumps his aptitude for scholarship. Gleefully deflowering what he terms Sophie's virginal naiveté concerning Jesus' and Mary Magdalene's true identities, Teabing gives an off-the-cuff overview of their mysterious history. His take doesn't hew to long-established facts but hey: nobody ever said *The Da Vinci Code* was the *Encyclopedia Britannica*.

Teabing cites two sources to shore up his account of ancient Christian doctrine: the Dead Sea Scrolls and what he calls "the Coptic Scrolls," both of which he identifies as suppressed "gospels" about the life of Jesus. In fact, the Dead Sea Scrolls never mention Jesus and contain no gospels. Furthermore, the "Coptic Scrolls" are not scrolls but leather-bound books, usually called the Nag Hammadi Library. Neither group of documents tells "the true Grail story," at least not the Teabing version. Most of the "suppression" of these documents did not stem from Vatican interference, as Teabing contends, but from academic and political infighting, black marketeering, and run-of-the-mill Middle East turmoil. Add to that some jaw-dropping carelessness (not deliberate censorship) on the part of the folks who stumbled on both caches of documents.

The Dead Sea Scrolls and the Nag Hammadi Library are two radically different sets of ancient religious texts from different countries, different traditions, and different centuries, written in different languages. However, they have a few key things in common. Both include doomsday-oriented ideas that can, at times, sound like a *Star Trek* plot. Both are partially concerned with secretive, separatist, fiercely antimaterialistic religious movements claiming a fast track to eternal salvation. Finally, both were accidentally discovered in the Middle Eastern desert in earthenware jars, in the mid-1940s, by guys named Mohammed.

The Dead Sea Scrolls

In 1947, when the Dead Sea was part of Jordan, a Bedouin shepherd named Mohammed "the Wolf" entered a cave on the sea's northwest shore near the Qumran ruins and found an ancient jug. Inside was a stash of antique scrolls made from animal skins and papyrus. Pretty sure that he had just won the lottery, Mohammed cut up some of the scrolls to sell them off, one shred at a time.

Over the next nine years, Bedouins, antiquities dealers, archaeologists, and black marketeers unearthed more than eight hundred manuscripts in eleven separate caves in the Judean desert. Some scrolls were intact. Others were scattered into thousands of fragments as small as a fingernail.

Written in Hebrew and Aramaic (the vernacular language of ancient Palestine), all the material was Jewish in content and was written between 250 B.C. and 70 A.D. The documents included the oldest known version of the Hebrew Bible, hymns, religious commentary, and scads of mystical texts. Most provocative, though, were manuscripts which many scholars believe pertain to the apocalyptic views and austere social order of a Jewish sect known as the Essenes. This group apparently followed a charismatic "Teacher of Righteousness" and segregated themselves from the rest of society to prepare for the imminent End of the World.

Early popular interest in the scrolls was stimulated by furious speculation that Christianity had been shown to be a direct offshoot of this Essene tradition. However, by 1991, when the texts became available to all scholars, the fever had largely relaxed into a more modest analysis. It's now thought that while Jesus and his followers may have shared many of the Essenes' purist views, what the Scrolls reveal is not the origin of Christianity but rather, previously unknown and important particulars about what Judaism itself was like at the dawn of Christianity.

Israel acquired the area around Qumran in the 1967 War, and today the Dead Sea Scroll collection is in Jerusalem's Israel Museum. There, scroll fragments are up for "adoption," as individual donors can contribute funds to preserve specific fragments.

The Nag Hammadi Library

In 1945, another Bedouin, Mohammed Ali, was digging for fertilizer on the banks of the Nile in Upper Egypt near the town of Nag Hammadi when he, too, found an ancient jar. Inside were thirteen leather-bound books produced around 350 A.D. and written in Coptic, the hieroglyphics-related language of pre-Islamic Egypt. The books were translations of Greek originals dating back two centuries. They comprised Christian and non-Christian texts, including purportedly "lost" gospels by several of Christ's apostles including Thomas, Peter, James, Philip, and, yes, Mary Magdalene, who is identified as Jesus' "companion."

The documents also include a smattering of Plato's *Republic* and a stack of spooky treatises with titles like "Thunder, Perfect Mind," and "The Testimony of Truth," which tells the Garden of Eden story from the snake's point of view.

According to one of the world's experts on these documents, Princeton University religion professor Elaine Pagels, whether any of them contain Jesus' authentic teachings is unknown. They do offer extraordinary insights into the diversity of the early Christian movement. Yes, Teabing was right to note that early orthodox Christian bishops did try to suppress this material as heresy—but they did so because it smacked of pantheism and because the manuscripts stemmed from a mystical tradition known as "Gnosticism," which departs from mainstream doctrine.

Basically, Gnosticism (from the Greek *gnosis* or "knowledge") is the doctrine of salvation by secret, intuitive knowledge. In fact, some of the Gnostic Gospels, as the Nag Hammadi Library is often called, appear to have as much in common with traditions like Buddhism and Zoroastrianism as they do with Christianity.

After many decades of academic haggling, the Nag Hammadi Library is finally available for all to read, and the originals repose at the Coptic Museum in Cairo.

THE BIG PICTURE: *THE LAST SUPPER*

Leonardo's *The Last Supper* has been reproduced so many times, on everything from refrigerator magnets to mouse pads, that it's easy to be blasé about it. But this over-familiar image has a radical past—even if you don't follow *The Da Vinci Code*'s theories.

Leonardo da Vinci was already an art star when, in 1495, Ludovico il Moro, of Milan's powerful Sforza family, commissioned his favorite artist to paint the refectory of Milan's Church of Santa Maria delle Grazie. It was a challenging assignment, not only because Ludovico was eager to see the project done quickly, but because Leonardo wasn't used to working on such a large scale (15 x 29 feet).

In the 15th century, Christian iconography was rigidly prescribed by the Roman Catholic church. Books like *Il Libro dell'Arte* (1437) provided practical guidelines on how to paint a Nativity, an Annunciation, or an Assumption. Rules for the use of symbols and attributes of holy figures were interpreted by the Church, and contemporary artists followed their lead.

But Leonardo, ever the maverick, chose his own path for his *The Last Supper*. Presenting the scene as a perfectly symmetrical stage set, Leonardo used perspective to bring the action into the foreground of the image. Receding lines, defined by the walls, coffered ceiling, and windows, dramatically focus the composition directly on the face of Jesus. A series of three windows at the back of the image, with a sfumato landscape beyond, serve as a light/dark device to throw the head of Christ into a sort of silhouette before a rectangular halo of natural light.

Christ is flanked by six of his apostles on each side, in two groups of three, all of whom respond to the startling news that one of them is about to betray their leader. Leonardo created a snapshot of one of the most dramatic moments in the New Testament. It was a groundbreaking juncture. Where traditionally the apostles' responses were dictated by stylized posturing, Leonardo's apostles express emotion through body language and facial expression. The you-are-there feeling of the painting is further enhanced by Leonardo's clever trick of lining up his entire cast of characters on one side of the table, as if facing a camera.

The Last Supper's Conservation

Usually when a needy work of art undergoes conservation, it's showered with compliments when the conservator's work is finished. When Leonardo's *The Last Supper* was unveiled after conservation, however, it set off shock waves. Conservator Pinin Brambilla Barcilon took a controversial approach; she chose to *conserve* what was left of Leonardo's original paint, rather than to *restore* the overall image to a cohesive whole. In fact, most of her work consisted of removing paint, applied in patch jobs during the course of five centuries, to restore the masterpiece to its original appearance.

You might think of a painting as a two-dimensional object, but conservators see flat paintings in 3-D. Microscopic cross-sections of paint layers help them understand the work's original makeup. They also reveal later additions by lesser artists. *The Last Supper*, as we had come to know it in the 20th century, was a regular layer cake of paint. Oil paint becomes brittle as it ages and tends to separate into small islands isolated by a network of cracks. Accelerated by the troublesome wall surface, Leonardo's original pigments had begun to flake off even during his lifetime. There were many subsequent attempts to reattach his paint and to fill in the gaps where it was missing. Barcilon faced a daunting hodgepodge of original bits covered over with a patchwork of restorers' additions.

The conservation lasted almost twenty years, from planning in the late 1970s through its completion in 1999. Working through a microscope, Barcilon removed everything that was not Leonardo's fragile original paint. The tiny paint fragments that were barely clinging to the wall were then firmly reattached. The remaining ghost of the original revealed such delights as a slice of orange on a plate (previously obscured by overpaint) and it brought to light the delicate brushwork in many of the original faces, which had not been seen for centuries.

Reviews of Barcilon's work were mixed, but many scholars now agree that revealing what little was left of the original painting was the way to go, even if the result was initially startling. (Barcilon did follow the standard practice of adding watercolor filler where the original paint was missing entirely, so the image remains cohesive.)

The characters' momentum is heightened by an important source of tension in the image—a knife, gripped in a hand, appears behind Judas's back, pointing toward Andrew, whose hands fly up. The most recent conservator makes a persuasive argument that this is Peter's hand and knife, somewhat awkwardly positioned since Peter's arm is akimbo as he leans forward to speak to John. Precisely what Leonardo intended may never be known, but this theory does hold water. Peter is historically the apostle who threatens the guard with a knife when Jesus is escorted away from this scene, and the gospel story was Leonardo's guide.

Leonardo's inventiveness didn't stop with the composition. He also tried out an untested technique—one which physically misfired. In the traditional *buon fresco* ("true fresco") method, pigments suspended in water were applied to fresh (*fresco*) lime plaster. Fresco painters have to work fast, finishing each section before the plaster dries. Leonardo experimented by coating the refectory's stone wall with a mix of gesso, pitch, and mastic, then applying his oil and tempera paints to the dry surface. This let him paint at his own pace and use more varied colors. But the paint didn't fully grip the surface and the mural began to deteriorate within 20 years of its completion. (*See* the sidebar on *The Last Supper*'s conservation *above* for details on the restoration.)

Acts of war and carelessness have also threatened the image: Allied bombs demolished the refectory in World War II, but sandbagging saved the painting. Jesus' feet, however, have been missing since a door was cut through the lower center portion of the wall in the 17th century. Art lovers whose accumulated moist breath threatens to kill the mural with kindness are now slowly pulsed into the refectory of Santa Maria delle Grazie every 15 minutes, with no more than 25 visitors at a time. *See* the On the Road With *The Da Vinci Code* chapter for details on visiting the painting.

THERE'S SOMETHING ABOUT MARY

Mary Magdalene and countless other female spiritual figures have long been associated with a force that can be described as the sacred feminine, the feminine aspects of a universal, pre-

Christian divinity. Teabing and Langdon describe this force, tied closely with the female ability to produce new life, as a "lost goddess." To the two scholars, Mary Magdalene is a particularly explosive embodiment of the sacred feminine.

As Teabing tries to convince Sophie of Mary Magdalene's extraordinary role, he explains that the divine Miss M. is worshipped "as the Goddess, the Holy Grail, the Rose, and the Divine Mother." Quite a tall order. Teabing also claims that after the Crucifixion, Mary Magdalene traveled to France, where she delivered a child, Sarah.

That's one version of the story. In another version Sarah was a gypsy queen residing in the south of France in a seaside village now called Stes-Maries-de-la-Mer. One day Sarah spotted a boat on the Mediterranean carrying three women. Sarah started taunting the women. Maybe she would have been more welcoming if she knew that these were holy women: Mary Magdalene; Mary Salome, the mother of John the Evangelist; and Mary Jacobe, a sister of the Virgin Mary.

Having just crossed 2,000 miles or so of the Mediterranean Sea in a boat that legends insist had neither sail nor oars, Mary Magdalene was travel-weary and stressed out. She stepped out of the boat onto the deep rough waters and invited Sarah to walk out to her. Sarah blithely stepped off the dock into the sea, where she nearly drowned. The multiple Marys hauled her in, saving her life.

It's an odd tale with many variations, but it may speak of the first meeting between paganism and Christianity. Whoever Sarah was—divine child, gypsy queen, pagan goddess—she, the Virgin Mary, and Mary Magdalene are considered manifestations of the sacred feminine.

The Goddess appears in art throughout (and even before) recorded history. Her image has been cropping up in some strange places, from a floor tile in a Mexican subway station to a grilled cheese sandwich sold on eBay and now on display at the online gambling site GoldenPalace.com. Paintings and statues depicting her have been credited with miraculous powers, particularly the dozens of mysterious, dark-skinned medieval statues known collectively as the black Madonnas.

Goddesses Through the Ages

*B*elow are a few examples of early goddesses from different cultures, representing a wide range of attributes and powers included in the "sacred feminine."

Prehistoric
Venus of Willendorf
This carving, created around 24,000-22,000 B.C., was found in 1908 in Austria. We'll likely never know if she represents a goddess or a real woman, though it's hard to imagine a woman in a hunter/gatherer society would be this curvy.

Egyptian
Bast
Goddess of joy, music, and dancing, she also protected against evil spirits. Until 1000 B.C. she was portrayed as a lioness. Her more docile cat side is a later development, as is her association with fragrance and her aromatic title "perfumed protector."

Greco-Roman
Athena
Goddess of war, wisdom, the arts, and justice. Athens, founded between 1400 and 1200 B.C., was named in her honor. Her symbols are the olive tree and the owl.

Indian
Saraswati

Goddess of knowledge, art, and music. According to the *Rig-Veda*, a Hindu holy book dated to 1500 B.C., she was once a river goddess. Saraswati's symbol is the lotus, which blooms from the mud. Her titles include "Dispeller of Darkness" and "Remover of Infatuations."

Celtic
Epona

Horse goddess of the Celtic Gauls, guardian of travelers and blacksmiths. Folk evidence pegs her rise before the Roman conquest of Gaul in 52 B.C. Often portrayed with a cornucopia, a symbol of fertility.

Chinese
Kuan Yin

Goddess of compassion and mercy. Buddhists believe that Kuan Yin will help anyone who speaks her name aloud. She was originally depicted as a male god. In 406 A.D., Buddhist monk Kumarajiva was the first to notice that Kuan Yin was (or is also) female.

Norse
Hel

Goddess of the underworld and the deceased, she is half alive and half dead and wears her bones on the outside of her skin. *Snorri's Edda,* a collection of poems collated around 1220 B.C., described the land that Hel rules as a cold and damp place.

Shady Ladies

Roughly half of the black Madonnas known to exist are in France. One, carved of dark wood and draped with brilliant beads and layers of colorful fabric, honors Sarah of Stes-Maries-de-la-Mer. Others are thought to represent the Virgin Mary, although some scholars believe all the black Madonnas depict pre-Christian goddesses.

A recent best-selling book, *The Secret Life of Bees,* centers on the black Madonnas. Its author, Sue Monk Kidd, said in an interview with *U.S. Catholic* magazine that she thought "there may have been a kind of underground nerve center for worshiping the divine feminine within the medieval church, and it often came through in the Black Madonna . . . we've got a very powerful amalgamation going on, a blending of the Christian Mary and these old earth goddesses."

Black Madonnas are often placed in the crypts and underground grottoes of churches, perhaps in recognition of the cave as a symbol of the earth mother. The black Madonna of Chartres, for instance, is housed in a grotto under the cathedral. According to legend, there was a grotto at this site with a statue of an ancient dark-skinned goddess giving birth, and Chartres cathedral was built right around the statue.

The Divine Miss M.

Although incorporating such localized examples of ancient sacred feminine images into Christian places of worship is not the norm, the remains of Mary Magdalene herself may straddle the divide between different kinds of consecrated ground.

Provençal folk tradition claims that Mary Magdalene spent the last years of her life in the French Alps, living in a cave now known as the Grotto of Ste-Baume, a spot with ancient associations of fertility goddesses. Her remains were reportedly housed in a basilica in the nearby village of St-Maximin, near Marseille. Her bones were supposedly removed and scattered during the French Revolution, but her head is said to remain in the cave at Ste-Baume. Both the basilica and the cave of Ste-Baume have been popular pilgrimage destinations for centuries. Kings, popes, and millions of faithful have visited, and on Mary Magdalene's feast day (July 22) a mass is held in the cave.

*An Arago disk marks the
Rose Line in the Palais Royal.*

Sophie and Langdon set a false trail at the Gare St-Lazare (top), an atmospheric train station that was a favorite of the Impressionists. The baffling cryptex that they try to crack has inspired custom-made "replicas" (above).

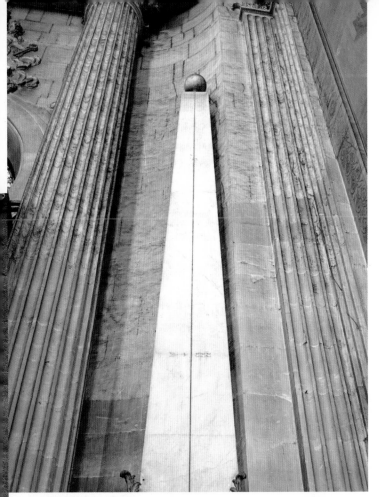

*The gilded line running
through St-Sulpice is part of
an 18th-century
"ecclesiastical compass."*

*Teabing's estate, the
17th-century Château
Villette, is a real-life
haven with stunning
Le Nôtre–style gardens.*

The figure of John in Leonardo's The Last Supper *(right) has drastically eroded. The most recent conservator noted that very little original paint is left in the robes and that nine-tenths of the original depiction of flesh is gone.*

Sophie moved closer to the image. The woman to Jesus' right was young and pious-looking, with a demure face, beautiful red hair, and hands folded quietly." —*The Da Vinci Code*

Bartholomew | James the Minor | Andrew | Judas | Peter | John | Christ | T

the Major
Philip

Matthew

Thaddeus

Simon

In his unprecedented composition, Leonardo shows emotion rippling through the Apostles as Jesus announces that one will betray him. Unlike preceding artists, Leonardo does not isolate Judas on one side of the table. Instead, Judas sits among the rest of the Apostles, though his face is the only one to be in shadow. His hand reaches inexorably towards a piece of bread, anticipating the moment when Jesus identifies him with a dipped morsel. John, by contrast, looks quite calm, safe in the knowledge that he is the disciple "whom Jesus loved" (John 13:23). Peter, leaning between Judas and John, bridges between the wicked and the good.

There is a long artistic tradition, particularly among quattrocento painters, of depicting John leaning on Christ during the Last Supper. This pose illustrates the gospel description of John being "close to the breast of Jesus" (John 13: 23). See, for example, the works of Barna da Siena (14th century, top left) and Jacopo Bassano (16th century, bottom left). John was also often shown asleep, a reference to his later sleep in the garden of Gethsemane, as in this

panel by Fra Angelico and his workshop (1450s, bottom right). After Leonardo's Supper, traditions loosened as artists tried new ways of representing the scene. In Tintoretto's version (1590s, top right), the table rakes along a dramatic diagonal and the group is surrounded by both serving maids and angels.

*Among the ancient
manifestations of the
sacred feminine are the
so-called "black Madonnas"
(top left) and the annual
pilgrimage festival of
Stes-Maries-de-la-Mer (top
right). Mary Magdalene,
seen by Teabing "as the
Goddess," has traditionally
been depicted as a penitent
sinner (Giotto at bottom
left, Georges de La Tour at
bottom right).*

Langdon races through the Palais Royal (above and right) on his way to the Louvre's inverted pyramid (following page). The hushed arcades in the Palais Royal evoke mystery and thrilling tension. (For more drama, either visit the neighboring theater, the Comédie Française, or see the movie Charade, *which ends with a chase sequence in the arcades.)*

How did history's bad girl become a saint venerated by so many?

Although it isn't explicitly stated in the Bible, many people believe that Mary Magdalene was a reformed prostitute. In the *Code*, Teabing asserts that the early Church actively promoted the idea of Mary Magdalene as a member of the world's oldest profession in order to destroy her potential power. She is described in the Gospel of Luke (Luke 8:2) as having been possessed by seven demons. Her bad rep was further compounded when she was associated with a woman who is identified only as one who "had lived a sinful life" (Luke 7:36-50) and anointed Jesus' feet with scented oil from an alabaster jar. Mary of Bethany is also cited as a woman who anoints Jesus with oil in John 11:2. Early church leaders morphed these women into one and Mary Magdalene's risqué reputation was sealed for the next fourteen centuries when Pope Gregory the Great said in a sermon in 591: "She whom Luke calls the sinful woman, whom John calls Mary [of Bethany], we believe to be the Mary from whom seven devils were ejected according to Mark."

The Catholic church issued an official statement in 1969 saying that Gregory slipped up in that sermon, but word of Mary Magdalene's rehabilitation still doesn't seem to have taken hold.

"From everything I've read on the subject, I'm inclined to think that Pope Gregory may have just made a mistake," says Lunaea Weatherstone, editor of *SageWoman* magazine, a publication devoted to the exploration of modern and ancient goddess lore. "But if Mary Magdalene had been portrayed as simply one of the close followers of Jesus, without any stain on her virtue, I think that it's very possible that women would have been treated with more honor in the church, as followers in the footsteps of Mary Magdalene," Weatherstone adds.

The Bible gives brief tantalizing glimpses of the woman who met Jesus when he expelled her demons and was at his side through tragedy and triumph. She stands at the foot of the cross with two other women, the male apostles having long fled the scene. She discovers Jesus' tomb is empty two days later; she is the first to learn of the Resurrection and is also the first to see Jesus alive again. But her place in church lore has long been focused on her role as a penitent sinner, despite some Christian writings that refer to her as "the apostle to the apostles."

Flawed or not, Mary Magdalene's reputation has an undeniable resonance, says Lesa Bellevie, author of *The Complete Idiot's Guide to Mary Magdalene*. "Mary Magdalene the repentant sinner had a profound influence on the direction taken by Western culture," Bellevie says. "As the Church's primary example of pious repentance, she became a tremendously popular saint."

"Mary Magdalene is a woman whose time has come," Bellevie believes. "We don't need to make up speculative histories for something to be spiritually meaningful, and neither does something need to be historically accurate for it to be spiritually meaningful—this is the power of mythology."

TALES OF THE CRYPTEX

In your hand you hold a cylinder crafted of white marble about the size of a can of Pringles® potato chips. It has five movable disks, each engraved with all of the letters of the alphabet. A secret message that you urgently need to read is stashed inside the hollow cylinder, but the only way to open this cryptex device is by carefully aligning the lettered disks to spell out a password.

Don't know the password? Too bad. You can't smash the cylinder against a rock or pry it open with a metal bar. The message hidden within is written on a thin sheet of papyrus curled around a delicate glass vial full of vinegar. Treat the cryptex harshly and the vial will shatter, the vinegar will leak out, and the papyrus and its message will dissolve in the liquid.

The cryptex, an invention that Dan Brown credits to Leonardo, seems like an idea that would have worked well during the Renaissance.

But experts agree that the device was unknown then. "I've studied the history of encryption and I'd know if someone during the Renaissance period had created a device like the one that's described in the book. Da Vinci did not invent any encryption device," says David Kahn, who taught military intelligence at Yale and Columbia universities and is currently on the Board of Advisors at the Spy Museum in Washington, D.C.

Kahn points out that an encryption device reminiscent of the cryptex was developed between 1790 and 1800 by Thomas Jefferson (his may have been based on an earlier device). Jefferson's "cipher-cylinder" consisted of wooden disks, each with a hole through its center. A randomized alphabet was carved around each disk's edge. The disks were then placed in a predetermined order on a spindle. To encode a message the sender lines up the disks to spell out the actual message, but then copies a line of random characters from another side of the device. To decode the message, the recipient lines up the disks on his cylinder to match the seeming gibberish in the ciphered message and examines the device to find a readable message.

Kahn believes Jefferson may have developed the device to circumvent the Black Chambers, groups of highly experienced codebreakers employed by England and other European countries. American revolutionaries relied heavily on codes to communicate during the war. Jefferson also used them when he served as America's minister to France in the 1780s, since European postmasters were known to read letters passing through their mail services.

A similar cylinder was invented around 1890 by a member of the French military, Etienne Bazarie. Bazarie's version used 30 separate disks and helped establish him as a leading cryptanalyst. The cylinder idea was resurrected once again shortly before World War I by the American military. An updated version of Jefferson's cipher-cylinder, made of metal and dubbed M-94, was widely used from 1921 to 1942 by the U.S. Army Signal Corps. "It was very effective for messages requiring low level security," says Kahn.

After appearing in *The Da Vinci Code,* the cryptex proved too attractive an idea to languish within the world of fiction. Modern "replicas" are available and have been used to present love notes, engagement rings, car keys, or tickets for a special vacation. Encrypta Gifts is one company that has designed new cryptexes for sale (www.encryptagifts.com). Justin Nevins, who sells custom-made cryptexes from his Web site (www.cryptex.org), says that after much research, he believes that while Leonardo might possibly have designed a similar device, it would have been nearly impossible to craft one out of marble.

Creating marble rings is difficult because of the stone's fragility. It tends to crack along its vein lines when stressed. Nevins said a marble cryptex exactly matching the one described in the book would require rings that are roughly 1/2 to 3/4 inch thick. This would result in either a cylinder too bulky to be comfortably held in someone's hand or an interior storage space of less than an inch—too small to be of any practical use.

"The technology and tools I developed to cut the marble thin enough to keep the box size manageable and the storage space as large as possible would not have been possible in da Vinci's time," Nevins says. Metal, however, would not be outside the realm of Leonardian possibility . . . .

leonardo:
renaissance
man

Portrait of the Artist as the "Great Enigma"

THE *CODE* DEPICTS a Leonardo da Vinci who's a far cry from the figure you might remember from Art History 101. In the novel, Leonardo helps guard information that would rock the foundations of Christianity. (First things first: he went by Leonardo, not *da Vinci*, which means "of Vinci," the town from which he came.) He's portrayed as a Grand Master of the Priory of Sion, a "flamboyant homosexual," a "prankster," and the "great enigma" for those on the Holy Grail trail. Not all of these characterizations have a basis in solid evidence; in fact, we know little of Leonardo's personal life. Mystery has always shrouded this Renaissance jack-of-all-trades.

EXPLORING RENAISSANCE ITALY

Although Leonardo was in many ways ahead of his time, he was also a product of his era—one of both unsurpassed innovation and great political instability. Between the mid-14th and 16th centuries, many factors converged to create the conditions for the Italian Renaissance. The Black Death ravaged Europe in the mid-1300s, killing approximately one-third of the population. Traditional social obligations slowly faded away as depression hit and peasants fled to new urban areas in Italy. Growing banking and commercial centers, based on economic diversification and technical innovation, spurred a new distribution of wealth, as well as shifts in power and social relations, the creation of rising merchant and capitalist classes—and a culture of patronage for all those starving young artists.

The burgeoning capitalist class coincided with some hefty religious and military events. When the Catholic Church relocated its headquarters from France to Rome, Italians saw some unique opportunities: first, to solidify the power of the Catholic Church; second, to unify Italy; and third, to revive the ancient glory of the Roman Empire. Easier said than done. The Holy Roman Empire and papacy constantly fought for control of the Italian peninsula. By the mid-1400s, the time of Leonardo's birth, the papacy, situated in Rome, exerted great power throughout Italy. Yet its hold over the peninsula was slowly waning as Italians started to question long-held beliefs and criticize Church practices, indiscretions, and extravagances. As complaints piled up, the Church grew more secular.

Unifying Italy also presented some problems. To make a long story short, between 1494 and 1559, the Italian city-states were constantly at war—amongst themselves and with France and Spain. These power struggles created some ugly situations: city-states and foreign rulers forged, betrayed, and reformed alliances. More important, as rulers constantly changed (don't assume any death was natural), the wars affected Leonardo's patrons and the spread of Renaissance ideals.

But while the wars ground on, there was a cultural growth spurt through a revival of Greco-Roman style and philosophy. The Renaissance affected all aspects of life in the tempestuous city-states: art, architecture, math, science, literature, religion, and philosophy. A major philosophical stream called humanism drew these fields together. Humanists looked back on the ancient literature of Socrates, Plato, Aristotle, and Homer; studied ancient Latin, Greek, and Hebrew texts; embraced science; questioned Christian teachings; reignited belief in the pagan gods; and rethought the relationship of the individual to him/herself, God, and society.

Florence, Leonardo's stomping ground, was a petri dish for these new ideas. Determined to showcase their up-and-coming city, the Medicis—the Florentine oligarchy and most powerful bankers in town—glorified their wealth and prestige by patronizing the arts. Early Renaissance artists like Giotto (1267–1337) had already moved on from the medieval style, substituting a new realism for the gold-clad, flat-faced Madonnas that characterized medieval art. In 1401, Florence's famous contest for a set of doors for the baptistery of its cathedral (or Duomo) officially ushered in Renaissance art. The Florentine Republic's competition attracted two major artists, Filippo Brunelleschi (1377–1446) and Lorenzo Ghiberti (1378–1455). Ghiberti won, and by 1424 (nearly 30 years before Leonardo's birth) he had finished a set of doors Michelangelo called the "Gates of Paradise." He combined fluid, classical figures with a realistic treatment of movement and detail; his use of perspective gave a remarkable sense of depth. (Don't feel badly for Brunelleschi, though—he went on to become the Renaissance's first great architect by building the cathedral's dome.) This work established Florence as the hub of artistic innovation, made artists more competitive and prominent, and produced a milieu that allowed the new Renaissance style to flourish. All this set the stage for Leonardo.

THE BIOGRAPHICAL NUTS & BOLTS

Paradox could have been Leonardo's middle name. Despite his unparalleled genius and fame, he never enjoyed lasting job security with any of the dukes or popes who employed him. He seems to have been a perfectionist as well as a procrastinator. Though he thought of himself as a painter above all else, he left only about two dozen paintings, many incomplete. He sketched hundreds of inventions in his notebooks, but few (if any) were built during his lifetime. And while those notebooks reveal much about his highly inventive mind, they disclose precious little about his personal life. Leonardo is thus the perfect poster boy for Dan Brown's novel of secrets and symbols.

He was a love child, born April 15, 1452 in either Anchiano or Vinci, neighboring towns just west of Florence in Tuscany, Italy. His father, Ser Piero da Vinci, was a prominent notary in Florence. His unwed mother, Caterina, probably worked in Ser Piero's household; a few historians even suggest she was a Christian convert who'd been a former slave in the Middle East. Although it's unclear who raised Leonardo, he may have spent his first few years with Caterina and then left for his father's house.

Much of what we know about Leonardo's personality has been deduced from what he wrote in his notebooks as well as from contemporaries like Giorgio Vasari's written observations. Early on, Leonardo exhibited the contradictory and unusual traits that marked his career. Charismatic and generous, fickle and distrustful of society, he was even a vegetarian, a practice highly unusual at the time. (Later, despite his pacifist nature, he designed military machines for the duke of Milan.) For such a genius, he wasn't raised or schooled as you might expect. Ser Piero's wife possibly taught him reading, writing, and some math, and he showed great talent with the *lira de braccio* (a precursor to the violin). Some scholars suggest his strange penmanship, his mirror-writing, resulted from his lack of schooling (*see* Leonardo's Codes, *below*). Leonardo never mastered geometry or the classical languages as a child; these he taught himself later in life. Instead, he learned from exploring the natural world around him. Since he was illegitimate, he couldn't attend university, and so was barred from professions like law or medicine. Leonardo's saving grace was that as a youth, he had shown great promise at drawing. When he was around 16, Ser Piero carted him off to apprentice with one of Florence's renowned artists and engineers, Andrea del Verrocchio (1435–88). Fortunately, this move coincided with the rise of the Medicis.

Workshop Days

A Florentine painter could never hope to gain fame and fortune unless he first joined an established artist's workshop (or *bottega*) with a master and his other apprentices. The workshop, part of a larger artists' guild, collaborated on commissioned pieces of art for patrons like the Church, the Medicis, or other ruling or wealthy families. In Verrocchio's workshop Leonardo learned the tricks of the trade: how to prepare wood panels, mix pigments, paint in

LEONARDO

tempera and oils, work in clay, cast bronze, and, of course, sweep floors. He also collaborated with others in the workshop, including Sandro Botticelli (1445–1510). Botticelli's name might ring a bell for something other than the *Birth of Venus*—in the novel, he was named as one of the Grand Masters of the Priory of Sion. Other colleagues included Pietro Perugino (1450–1523) and Domenico Ghirlandaio (1449–94), both known for their Sistine Chapel frescoes. During his tenure with Verrocchio, Leonardo contributed to different commissions and undertook some independent works, including *Annunciation* (c. 1475–78); *Landscape of Santa Maria della Neve* (1473), praised for its perspective, emotion, and light values; and *Baptism of Christ* (c. 1472–75). In the latter, Leonardo painted such a realistic angel that, according to Vasari, Verrocchio swore never to pick up a paintbrush again.

Leonardo's apprenticeship probably ended around 1472, when he joined the artists' guild. Still, he remained with Verrocchio before pursuing an independent career—and, during this time, experienced some of his most difficult years. Scholars have long questioned Leonardo's sexuality. While Leonardo certainly wasn't the flamboyant homosexual that Langdon describes, his sexual orientation is still up for debate. In 1476, while possibly living in Verrocchio's household, Leonardo was denounced for acts of sodomy. Despite Italians' fascination with classical Greek mythology and homoerotic male love, Florence adhered to strict sexual mores and severely punished homosexual relations. Leonardo thus marched to trial. Though acquitted, he probably spent some lonely time in confinement.

Striking Out on His Own

Comments written in his notebooks indicate that these events put Leonardo in a deep funk. But the setback didn't mar his career. In 1476, Leonardo set up his own bottega in Florence, probably in the Santissima Annunziata convent, which rented space to artists. Leonardo, though he never married, adopted a couple of apprentices of his own, Francesco Melzi and Gian Giacomo Caprotti da Oreno, known as Salai ("little Satan"), who stayed with him until his death. During Leonardo's first Florentine period, he received a few commissions and even some interest from Lorenzo de' Medici's court, though not enough to ensure him a coveted position as court artist. He painted the *Portrait of Ginevra de' Benci* (c.

1474); *Madonna and Child* (c. 1473), also known as *Madonna with the Carnation*; the unfinished *St. Jerome* (c. 1480–83); and *Adoration of the Magi* (c. 1481–82), which he abandoned as well. By the late 1470s, Leonardo had established himself as a painter of some renown—and much flakiness. But greater opportunities awaited.

The Italian Wars had messed things up quite a bit, and Leonardo had to adapt to the times. In 1482, he wrote to Ludovico Sforza (1452–1508), the Duke of Milan (better known as "Il Moro" for his dark complexion), applying for the position of military engineer. Leonardo's skills as artist came as an afterthought. Sforza feared invasion from enemies of all kind, especially Venice and France. As he suspected, he'd eventually find himself caught in the mayhem. But when Leonardo arrived in Milan in 1482, the city was momentarily safe. Since Sforza no longer needed an engineer, he capitalized on Leonardo's artistic talents, which he had heard much about and had possibly witnessed on a previous visit to Florence. Leonardo ran his own workshop, dabbled in anatomy and church architecture, and organized court pageants (not his first choice, but at least he got to invent puzzles to amuse the audience). He also, of course, drew combat tools, canals, and fortresses, but these were never built.

One of his greatest projects entailed constructing a bronze equestrian statue for Ludovico's father, Francesco Sforza. After studying horses' anatomy and movements, Leonardo started work around 1489, building a clay model of a rearing horse 23 feet high and weighing almost 80 tons. But, because he procrastinated too long, his efforts didn't pan out. In 1494, the French invaded Milan and the bronze earmarked for the equestrian memorial was made into cannons. Leonardo's project sputtered on; nearly 15 years later, he designed, though never finished, a similar monument for the tomb of Marshal Gian Giacomo da Trivulzio. In 1999—500 years later—the sculptor Nina Akamu designed an 8-foot, 15-ton model manufactured in bronze by the Tallix Art Foundry in New York. Her sculpture, now at the San Siro Hippodrome in Milan, is based on her studies of Leonardo's writings and his sketches for the never-completed bronze.

During his Milanese stint, Leonardo continued making a name for himself by painting some of his most famous works: the two versions of *The Madonna of the Rocks* (1483–86, c. 1495–1508); *Lady with an Ermine* (c. 1496?); *Portrait of a Musician* (c. 1482–

LEONARDO

90); *Madonna Litta* (c. 1490); and the decorated ceiling of Sforza's castle, *Sala delle Asse* (c. 1496). And he started his most famed (and doomed) painting of all, *The Last Supper* (1495–98), in the refectory of the Dominican convent of Santa Maria delle Grazie in Milan (*see* the History Lessons chapter). But, in 1499, Milan fell to the French, spelling potential disaster for Sforza's court artist at the peak of his career.

On the Road Again

Ludovico Sforza had been Leonardo's greatest supporter and patron; with Louis XII's invasion, Leonardo started afresh. Around 1500 he returned to Florence—and found an unfamiliar city. The Medicis had been exiled; Charles VIII's French army now occupied the streets; and the Pisans had decided to mutiny. Although the wretched political situation did nothing to help Leonardo's career, he still accepted a commission from some friars for a painting of Madonna, Saint Anne, and the infant Christ. Known today as the *Burlington House Cartoon* (c. 1499–1500), this chalk drawing was never completed. Around 1508–10, Leonardo painted an oil version of the scene, *The Virgin and Child with St. Anne* (c. 1508–13?), now considered a masterpiece. (Well, aren't they all?)

Before he could complete any of his ongoing projects, Leonardo took another career detour. In the summer of 1502, Leonardo, who was rapidly becoming the consummate consultant, went to work as a military engineer for the treacherous General Cesare Borgia (1475–1507). Although he called himself a pacifist, Leonardo could not afford to reject a perfectly good job; he also reasoned that his work might somehow help bring about peace. The illegitimate son of Pope Alexander VI, Borgia was heading the military campaign to join together the battling Italian states under one Papal State—the Church. Leonardo traveled with Borgia for a year throughout central Italy. Along the way, he befriended Niccoló Machiavelli (1469–1527), secretary of the Florentine Republic and author of *The Prince* (1513), who later helped Leonardo acquire some commissions. Leonardo also designed a bridge to span the Golden Horn in Constantinople for ambassadors of the Ottoman Empire during this time. The single-span, triple-arch stone bridge, nearly 800 feet long and 75 feet wide, would have been the longest in the world, if it had been built. In 1995, a Norwegian artist, using Leonardo's blueprint, designed a miniature copy, a pedestrian crossing, in the town of Aas (near Oslo), proving the value of Leonardo's engineering skills to modern times.

In 1503, sick of the violence that Borgia left in his wake, Leonardo returned to Florence. Back in his old haunts, Leonardo matched wits and skills with Michelangelo (1475–1564) for the first time. Leonardo's rival, a sculptor, architect, and painter, would become most famous for painting the Sistine Chapel's fresco ceiling and *The Last Judgment* over the altar, and for sculpting hyper-real renditions of David and Moses. Unlike Leonardo, Michelangelo curried favor with the Medici clan and enjoyed the patronage of Pope Julius II and Pope Leo X in Rome. Michelangelo also ridiculed Leonardo's procrastination. Circumstances brought them together in 1503 (the year Leonardo started his most famous portrait, the *Mona Lisa*), when the two found themselves working side by side on murals for the Council Hall's great hall in honor of the Republic of Florence. Leonardo, though he may not have felt completely at ease with the younger artist, nonetheless expressed admiration for the powerful figures bursting with tension and emotion that embodied Michelangelo's High Renaissance style. Had either painter finished his mural of victorious military battles in Florence's recent history—Leonardo's depicting the Battle of Anghiari, Michelangelo's the Battle of Cascina—two masters' paintings would have coexisted. But Michelangelo was called away by Pope Julius II and Leonardo left for Milan.

The French Connection

This time, Charles d'Amboise, the French governor of Lombard, had invited Leonardo to Milan to work for Maximilian Sforza, Ludovico's son and the present Duke of Milan. From 1506 on, Leonardo enjoyed a freedom (and salary) he had not previously experienced. Paid by the French, he continued the anatomical studies he'd begun in Florence, believing they would be his greatest contribution to humankind. He also tried to wrap up other projects. Unfortunately, these halcyon days ended when Charles d'Amboise died in 1511, and the uneasy peace between Maximilian Sforza and the French king came to an abrupt end. Leonardo's job had once again become a wartime casualty.

Leonardo had not rubbed shoulders successfully enough with the powerful Medicis to ensure a lasting or profitable relationship with them. They had instead lavished their attention on Michelangelo, Botticelli, and Raphael (1483–1520). The latter, an outstanding painter, adopted Leonardo's and Michelangelo's artistic innovations and, along with them, formed the great High Renaissance triad. In 1513, Leonardo strove for a connection with Prince Giuliano de' Medici, one of the late Lorenzo's sons. The Medicis were "in" again in Florence, and Giuliano's brother, Giovanni, had become Pope Leo X. Leonardo and his two students thus settled in the Vatican's Belvedere. Despite this honor, Leonardo never worked at length for the Vatican as did Raphael, nor did he fill the hundreds of commissions from the Vatican that Langdon mentions. His stint there did give him time to experiment with flight, botany, anatomy, optics, oil paints, and irrigation techniques in the marshes south of Rome. He probably started *St. John the Baptist* (c. 1513–16) during this time as well.

> **LEO SAYS**
>
> "When fortune comes seize her with a firm hand. In front, I counsel you, for behind she is bald."

Leonardo's fortune changed again all too soon. When the French king Louis XII died in 1515, his baby-faced cousin, François I, invaded Milan and tried to oust Maximilian Sforza. Giuliano de' Medici entered the fray and was killed, robbing Leonardo of yet another employer. But somewhere, somehow, Leonardo had met the new French king, François I. In line with what had become a consulting career, Leonardo accepted a generous invitation to the French court. In 1516, he moved into the humble castle of Cloux (or Clos Lucé), connected to the king's royal château at Amboise, in the Loire Valley. Unable to paint after suffering a paralyzing stroke, the aging Leonardo embarked on other projects: organizing his soon-to-be-reorganized notebooks, planning an irrigation project south of the Loire, drawing a royal palace at Romorantin, and constructing a mechanical lion. This cushy arrangement seemed to suit both artist and patron alike. François, who clearly recognized Leonardo's genius, apparently found him a most stimulating companion and philosopher.

Growing more ill and frail, Leonardo died on May 2, 1519—rumor has it in the arms of the king. Initially buried in the cloister of St-Florentine in Amboise, Leonardo's remains were eventually transferred to one of the castle's chapels. Today, visitors can pay their respects to Leonardo's restored tomb, which resides in the

Chapel of St. Hubert on the castle grounds. (See the On the Road with *The Da Vinci Code* chapter for more details on visiting Amboise.)

LEONARDO'S CODES

Before Dan Brown's book was published, any discussion of a "da Vinci code" would probably not have included an esoteric analysis of the master's paintings. The big mystery that sparked centuries of debate and speculation was Leonardo's unusual handwriting.

Leonardo typically started writing on the right side of a page and moved to the left, producing script that was reversed, as if reflected in a mirror. Some think he did this to keep people from easily deciphering his writings. But most experts now believe that rather than trying to make his writings illegible, Leonardo wrote in mirror-script to ensure that his words *would* be readable.

"Leonardo was working fast, on a small scale with very smudgeable material," says Martin Kemp, professor of the history of art at the University of Oxford and author of the acclaimed biography *Leonardo*. The smudgeable substance Kemp refers to is the red chalk Leonardo often used. A left-handed person writing left to right would have smeared the chalk as his hand moved across the page.

Kemp adds that the mirror-script does not in itself make Leonardo's writing all that difficult to read. "It's just that he writes very badly in a horrible late-mediaeval hand," says Kemp.

When Leonardo was writing notes about sensitive matters, he didn't rely on mirror-script to provide privacy. Instead he spelled a few key names backward. Kemp says that Leonardo employed this simple cipher only three times, once in notes to himself about a secret trip he made to Rome with the Count of Ligny—cousin of Louis XII who invaded Milan in 1499, staking claim to the city ruled by Leonardo's patron Ludovico Sforza—and twice when recording recipes for painting materials.

Three uses of a weak cipher in thousands of pages of notes certainly doesn't point to a man who was manic about privacy. But

LEONARDO

Leonardo & Religion

hile Bezu Fache claims that Leonardo "had a tendency toward the darker arts" of pagan beliefs, Langdon counters that Leonardo "was an exceptionally spiritual man, albeit one in constant conflict with the Church." While we have few firsthand indications of Leonardo's religious leanings, Langdon's idea is likely closer to the truth.

Most historians believe that Leonardo was Catholic. He owned a copy of the Bible. Yet he sometimes bucked Church teachings; his human dissections, for example, challenged Church law. Though the Church was growing more secular, scientific inquiry (under some popes, anyway) was still heresy. Leonardo also believed that the institution of the Church was corrupt because of the sale of indulgences and emphasis on money.

In his notebooks, Leonardo mused on God as supreme designer. But since God was not a product of experience (or provable through empirical knowledge), he/she/it must be a more holistic divinity. In the end, it seems that Leonardo created his own brand of religion that honored respect for all life over a God on high.

---

the idea that Leonardo believed he had something to hide has been around for hundreds of years.

A note scribbled on what was once part of the binding of the *Codex Leicester* reads "Vinci used to write in a left-handed manner . . . it could be read rather easily by means of a large mirror; it is probable that he did this so that not all could read his writings so easily." Experts believe this note was written sometime between 1690 and 1717, possibly by the Roman painter Giuseppe Ghezzi, who in 1690 discovered the long-lost text stashed in a storage trunk in Rome. The note helped fuel the idea of Leonardo's purposeful penmanship.

But in the essay "Leonardo, Left-Handed Draftsman and Writer," author Carmen Bambach surveys scholars of Leonardo's time and our own and concludes that "for Leonardo, his manner of writing was clearly one of practicality."

Still, Leonardo probably got a little thrill out of mystifying people with his odd penmanship. He liked pranks. According to a

1550 biography by Vasari, Leonardo once kept an odd-looking lizard as a pet. He decided the creature should be further customized and made wings, horns, and a beard that he fastened to the animal.

For his own and his friends' amusement, Leonardo also enjoyed creating rebuses, word puzzles that use images to represent words or parts of words. His rebuses appear on several notebook pages that are now part of the art collection at Windsor Castle. The easiest one for an English reader to understand contains the letter *O* and a sketch of a pear (*pera* in Italian), a rebus for "opera." Cute, but hardly the stuff of sophisticated code making.

Which is not to say that there aren't concealed communications in Leonardo's work. Like other Renaissance artists, Leonardo sometimes included oblique references to the identities of the people in his portraits. In the background of one portrait Leonardo includes a large juniper tree. The Italian word for juniper, *ginepro*, alludes to the first name of the lady portrayed: Ginevra de' Benci. In another portrait, Cecilia Gallerani is shown holding a white ermine, *galee* in Greek, and a reference to the sitter's last name.

But the meaning attributed to the title *Mona Lisa* in *The Da Vinci Code* is a fictional construct. Langdon claims that Mona Lisa is an anagram of the names of the Egyptian gods of fertility: Amon (male) and L'isa (Isis, female), Leonardo's coded reference to "the divine union of male and female." The anagram technically works, but Leonardo never titled the painting and it wasn't known as the *Mona Lisa* until decades after his death. Around 1550, Vasari identified the subject as Lisa Gherardini, wife of a wealthy Florentine merchant. Prior to Vasari's identification, the painting now known to much of the world as the *Mona Lisa* was described in several letters and inventory notes only as a portrait of "a courtesan in a gauze veil."

LEONARDO

Magnificent Obsession

*L*angdon's first glimpse of the *Codex Leicester* (pronounced "lester") is described in *The Da Vinci Code* as a disappointment. The source of his distress: Leonardo's neatly written pages were totally incomprehensible.

Even if you're fluent in medieval Italian, the *Codex Leicester* isn't an easy read. Leonardo's famous backwards script is difficult to decipher. Happily, it doesn't take a mirror and a linguist's skill to enjoy the hundreds of sketches scribbled on the pages. Among them is an illustration of a device that one museum's exhibition catalogue described as "curiously similar to a modern espresso machine."

There are 10 known codices created from Leonardo's thousands of manuscript pages. The *Codex Leicester* is comprised of 18 linen (not parchment, as stated in *The Da Vinci Code*) paper sheets folded into 72 pages. Leonardo was in his fifties and living in Milan when he filled these pages. Working on sheets of loose paper, he put down his theories about water, astronomy, fossils, and hydraulics.

After Leonardo's death, his student Francesco Melzi guarded his mentor's files until his own death in 1570. Melzi's heirs then sold single sheets of Leonardo's work to anyone who expressed an interest. In 1630, sculptor Pompeo Leoni collected many of the pages but then decided to act as Leonardo's editor, reorganizing the material by subject matter instead of by date. Creating coherent notebooks from Leonardo's loose sheets of paper probably seemed like a swell idea at the time, but the codices now lack context.

The *Codex Leicester* is named for Thomas Coke, the Earl of Leicester, who bought it in 1717 from painter Giuseppe Ghezzi, who found it in 1690 while cleaning out a storage room in Rome. American businessman Armand Hammer purchased the *Codex Leicester* in 1980 for just under $6 million and promptly renamed it the *Codex Hammer*. Hammer decided to build his own museum to display the codex, but he died three weeks after the Armand Hammer Museum and Cultural Center opened in 1990. His estate was mired in legal problems, and the *Codex Hammer* was sold in 1994 to Microsoft's Bill Gates for $30.8 million. Gates restored the codex's original name.

When not on loan to museums, the *Codex Leicester* resides in Gates's Medina, Washington mansion in a customized lightproof and climate-controlled vault.

PAINTING A PICTURE OF LEONARDO'S ART

Leonardo considered himself first and foremost a painter, an occupation that brought together the "universal" sciences (including mathematics, optics, and anatomy) that interested him most. Although he didn't invent realism in painting, Leonardo epitomized all the advances Renaissance artists made between the 1400s and the High Renaissance of the early 1500s. During this period, painters devised ways to represent three-dimensional figures and objects on a two-dimensional surface in a way that conveyed distance and depth. Three Renaissance greats influenced Leonardo's techniques: Donatello (1386–1466) in sculpture, Brunelleschi in architecture, and Masaccio (1401–28) in painting. Each sought to perfect mathematical laws of proportion to create realistic, intensely human forms.

From Leonardo's notebooks, it's clear that he intended to write treatises on almost every subject he studied, including painting. He started a *Treatise on Painting* (or *Trattato della Pittura*) for his students in Milan, possibly at Ludovico Sforza's request. The work, published in 1651 in Paris, more than a century after Leonardo's death, contains his notes on perspective; composition; expression of emotions; the human form; effects of light, shadow, and color; and the profession of the artist.

Leonardo believed that everything in the world, from the stars to the human body, could be boiled down to mathematical and scientific truths. Never proficient in math as a youth, Leonardo picked up important lessons from the Franciscan monk Luca Pacioli (1445–1517), an expert on Euclidean geometry whom he met in the Court of Milan. The great Italian architect and art theorist Leon Battista Alberti (1404–72) had already expounded on perspective, but Leonardo's *Treatise on Painting* and his experiments with a pinhole camera further justified linear perspective. In one of the best illustrations of perspective, *The Last Supper*, viewers' eyes go straight to Jesus (*see* the History Lessons chapter). But Leonardo didn't always get things right. In his early study for *Adoration of the Magi* (c. 1481), the figures and the background ruins don't add up to a coherent whole, since some of the animals and people (including the Virgin and child) appear out of proportion in relation to their decrepit architectural surroundings. (Nitpicking, really—for its time, the *Adoration*'s perspective was unparalleled.) In his *Treatise* Leonardo also discussed the perspective of color, the idea that colors weaken as they recede from the eye. In the *Mona Lisa*, the hills just behind Lisa are reddish-brown; they assume a cooler hue as they move farther into the distance. Leonardo also wrote about the perspective of disappearance, the idea that objects in a painting should appear vaguer as they seem to move farther away from the eye.

Leonardo also achieved a new realism in painting by using three techniques he didn't invent, but perfected to an unusual degree: chiaroscuro, sfumato, and contrapposto. First was the problem of lighting; we can perceive many colors and ranges of brightness that paints can't replicate exactly. Medieval artists splashed their work with light colors like gold over darker objects to achieve a three-dimensional effect, but these special effects didn't add up to a realistic sense of depth. All those medieval Madonnas, despite the light colors that indicate folds of cloth, look rather flat. But Leonardo understood how to use light and shadow to create the illusion of depth. He used a technique called chiaroscuro (meaning "light" and "dark" in Italian) to contrast light and shade in a painting and define forms. For example, in *St. John the Baptist*, St. John emerges from dense shadows into a pool of godly light without actually having an outlined form.

Leonardo also used sfumato (*see* the Sfumato sidebar *in* the Paris Chapter) to achieve some semblance of reality by blurring lines and merging colors rather than outlining the contours of figures. The backgrounds and faces in *Ginevra de' Benci* and *Mona Lisa*, for example, seem to melt into each other rather than exhibit harsh outlines. Leonardo's use of easily manipulated oil paint, just starting to come into vogue, augmented this effect.

Finally, in his portraits Leonardo also discarded the stiff, frontal pose of sitters by giving them some mobility, which also enhanced the illusion of depth. He modeled human figures according to contrapposto, "counterpoise," or "balance." The hips and legs turn in different directions from the shoulders and the head, and the weight of the body presses unevenly on the feet. This technique, which Leonardo used in many of his paintings, including *Leda and the Swan* (c. 1505–10), gave figures a more realistic appearance—and personality. Again, Leonardo did not pioneer this technique. It was used in ancient Greek sculpture, then reappears again in Donatello's sculptures and Masaccio's paintings.

Leonardo proportioned his figures by applying mathematical and geometrical concepts to the human body. Like other Renaissance artists, he pursued the idea of Divine Proportion, or golden mean—the concept that natural objects have a perfect proportion that achieves harmony and balance. Of course, no one, not even Leonardo, applied this idea perfectly. Still, it guided everything he did, from studying the human skull to painting the table in *The Last Supper*. Of course, proportion is all about shapes, too, not just ratios. So, in many of his paintings Leonardo organized figures and space in order to create pleasing, geometrically harmonious compositions. His pyramidal composition, in *The Virgin and Child with St. Anne,* for example, gives a sense of harmony and proportion—even if no one's exactly sure who's holding up the Virgin!

> **LEO SAYS**
>
> "A painter is not admirable unless he is universal."

Even in his use of iconography Leonardo distinguished himself. He more or less adhered to traditional religious themes that ensured him meal tickets, but still shook things up a bit. Despite the revival of classical antiquity and interest in pagan gods, many patrons still wanted Christian themes. In the name of realism, Leonardo didn't use the gold that had brightened up pasty Renaissance pieces and he withheld halos from many of his Madonnas. Still, he wasn't above using some traditional Christian symbolism. The dove hovering above Christ's head in *Baptism of Christ* represents the Holy Ghost. In the first version of the *Madonna of the Rocks*, the columbine beside the Virgin's face represents her love for the Holy Spirit; the ivy denotes chastity; and the blood-red anemone, a flower of death, foreshadows the Crucifixion.

In his portraits—a form of painting that came into vogue with the Renaissance and loosening grip of the Church—Leonardo also mixed innovation with the tried-and-true. In *Lady with an Ermine (Cecilia Gallerani),* his subject sits in an anatomically correct three-quarters pose, cast in a light that illuminates her milky complexion. Leonardo hinted at the sitter's identity by placing a white ermine, the symbol of nobility, in her lap. The Greek word for ermine is *galee*, alluding to her name, Cecilia Gallerani. A wink and a nod.

LEONARDO

Q&A with Martin Kemp

*M*artin Kemp is Professor of the History of Art at the University of Oxford and author of the biography *Leonardo*.

Q: Would people in Leonardo's time have seen him as an artistic superhero, as we do now?

A: There are signs that contemporaries recognized something extraordinary in Leonardo . . . the clearest evidence of the awe in which he was held was his treatment in the last years of his life by Francis I, king of France, who set up Leonardo with a fine manor house and huge salary. Francis was reported as saying that no one knew as much as Leonardo.

Q: Leonardo frequently made his living as a consultant. Do you think he resented being pulled away from his art in order to make a living?

A: I sense that he relished putting his knowledge to use at a high level, acting as an expert on subjects across an unrivalled range of arts, sciences, and technology. If there is a frustration apparent in his notebooks, it involves the impossibility of not being able to do everything simultaneously. There is a repetitive doodle in his notebook that reads, "Tell me if anything were ever done?"

Q: How would Leonardo have described himself?

A: Leonardo would, first and foremost, have described himself as a painter. He believed that painting was the supreme "science," since it involved the most complete understanding of visual things if the artist was to re-make nature perfectly, acting as if a god. Everything else sprang from visual knowledge. . . . He could not have called himself either a "scientist" or an "artist," since these were not terms current in his day. I am sure he would have liked the later tag of *uomo universale* ("universal man").

Q: What religious ideas resonated with Leonardo?

A: Every wonder he saw in nature declared that there must be a supreme "designer" at work. This "designer" was identified as God, but the very nature of God was not susceptible to rational investigation since he was beyond finite comprehension. This was not a new attitude, but he pushed the separation between them as far as anyone. . . . It is notable that alone of the great Renaissance thinkers he never expressed any opinions on theological matters. He was in the business of knowledge and its representation, not faith.

Visiting Leonardo's Works

Travelers out and about in the world will surely stumble across a Leonardo or two; here's where his known paintings reside. The workshop production of several paintings means that only certain parts of those paintings (like one of the angels in the *Baptism of Christ*) can safely be identified as Leonardo's work.

Alte Pinakothek (Munich, Germany)
Madonna with the Carnation (c. 1473?, partial contribution)
Biblioteca Ambrosiana (Milan, Italy)
Portrait of a Musician (c. 1482–90, authorship uncertain)
Convent of Santa Maria delle Grazie (Milan, Italy)
The Last Supper (c. 1495–98)
Czartoryski Museum (Cracow, Poland)
Lady with an Ermine (c. 1496?)
The Hermitage (St. Petersburg, Russia)
Madonna Benois (c. 1478?, authorship uncertain)
Madonna Litta (c. 1490, partial contribution)
The Louvre (Paris, France)
Annunciation (c. 1475–78?, partial contribution)
Bacchus (Saint John the Baptist in the Desert) (c. 1510–15, partial contribution)
Battle of Anghiari (Leonardo's chalk drawing, c. 1503–05; copy by Peter Paul Rubens, c. 1603)
La Belle Ferronière (c. 1495–99?, at least partial contribution)
Mona Lisa (c. 1503–1506?)
Portrait of Isabella d'Este (c. 1499, unfinished)
St. John the Baptist (c. 1513–16, mostly Leonardo with some later additions)
The Virgin and Child with St. Anne (c. 1508–13?, unfinished)
Madonna of the Rocks (first version, c. 1483–86)
National Gallery (London, England)
Burlington House Cartoon (c. 1499–1500)
Virgin of the Rocks (second version, c. 1495–1508)
National Gallery of Art (Washington, D.C.)
Portrait of Ginevra de' Benci (c. 1474?)
Private Collections
Madonna with the Cat (c. 1480, authorship uncertain), Savona, Italy
Madonna with the Yarnwinder (c. 1501–10), Drumlanrig, Scotland

LEONARDO

Salvator Mundi (c. 1506–13, authorship uncertain), Paris
The Uffizi Gallery (Florence, Italy)
Adoration of the Magi (c. 1481–82, unfinished)
Baptism of Christ (c. 1472–75, partial contribution)
Leda and the Swan (c. 1505–10)
Vatican Museum (Rome, Italy)
St. Jerome (c. 1480–83, unfinished)

ENGINEERING INGENUITY

Leonardo probably started fooling around with various machines when he entered Verrocchio's workshop. When he died, he left behind about 15,000 drawings of almost everything under the sun: a machine for making rope; an automated trench digger; a machine for making mirrors; a lifting jack; twin-armed cranes; a multiple-cylinder mill; a fabric stretcher; a spring-powered clock; and many, many more. Unfortunately, most of Leonardo's inventions never saw the light of day during his lifetime. On his deathbed, he reputedly begged François I to tell him if any of his designs had been built—or if he had toiled in vain.

Since Leonardo kept most of his notebooks private, it's unknown whether his contemporaries realized the extent of his creativity. In fact, other inventors reinvented some of his contraptions after his death. That many of Leonardo's inventions would not have worked hardly diminishes his accomplishments. Some, including his crowning achievement—his flight machines—were impractical due to the limits of the human- and animal-driven power sources available at the time.

The Wave of the Future

Nonetheless, today Leonardo's machines are as valuable for their pioneering designs as they are for insights into his mind. Who else would have conceived of the principles behind a car in the fifteenth century? Around 1478 Leonardo designed a forerunner to the modern car—a rather sophisticated three-wheeler, no license required. After someone wound up the pair of back wheels, the vehicle, a boxy, open-top structure, was supposed to spring forward. The third wheel acted as a rudder. Unfortunately, the spring system didn't work as planned, but Leonardo's sketch of the carriage's transmission reveals a complicated variable speed drive. In the late 1990s, Italian professor Carlo Pedretti and American robotic scientist Mark Rosheim collaborated on a working model of the car. After some confusion over Leonardo's original design, *Leonardo's Fiat*, a 5 x 5½-foot box-frame wagon, really moved—100 feet!

Leonardo may also have sketched another, more practical vehicle: the bicycle. In the 1960s, a drawing of a bike was found in one of Leonardo's notebooks, the *Codex Atlanticus*. The rather unsophisticated drawing illustrates a two-wheeler with a wooden frame, pedals, handlebars, a chain drive, and rear sprocket. However, controversy exists over whether or not Leonardo actually invented this design, or if others, over the years, tampered with the notebook and sketched it in.

Although we know from comments written in his notebooks that Leonardo was a pacifist, he sketched a vast array of military machines for Ludovico Sforza. Yes, Leonardo's inventions did include the horrific weapons of war that Dan Brown claims—but none for torture. His military machines included armored tanks, battering rams, scaling ladders, the submarine, hull rammers, rapid-firing crossbows, front-loading firearms, a 33-barreled machine gun, scythed chariots, diving gear, lagoon dredges, canals, and bridges. One of Leonardo's more interesting projects involved changing the course of the Arno River away from Pisa, a plan he devised with Machiavelli while traveling with Borgia through central Italy. The rerouted river would supposedly decrease the threat of invasion from Pisa, help irrigate Tuscany, and make the river more navigable. Leonardo's project never came to fruition, but 20th-century anti-flooding measures along the Arno resemble Leonardo's designs quite a bit.

Taking Flight

A flying machine, however, was Leonardo's most persistent dream. Over his lifetime, he drew many models of flight machines, applying the physiological principles he observed in birds and bats to human-powered aviation. Since Leonardo believed that the world operated according to universal laws of dynamics, he believed an engineered human wing would do the trick quite nicely. Many of the wing structures he planned used light, flexible

The Prankster Goes Pop

*L*eonardo, a trickster all his life, played plenty of clever practical jokes on his friends. According to Giorgio Vasari, he produced a painted Medusa-like figure out of dead animals to scare his father and once inflated pigs' intestines to fill a room. But Leonardo has been on the receiving end of some jokes and irreverencies as well—many involving his favorite painting, the *Mona Lisa*. After all, fame breeds familiarity, no?

Among the most celebrated of copies, **Marcel Duchamp**'s Dada-inspired 1919 *L.H.O.O.Q.* (reading the initials aloud sounds like the French phrase for "she has a hot ass") depicts *Mona Lisa* with a mustache and goatee.

In his 1954 *Self Portrait as Mona Lisa*, Surrealist artist **Salvador Dalí** added his mustache (and other personal features) to his mock-up of Mona.

Pop artist **Andy Warhol** multiplied Mona's face many times over in his 1963 serigraph, *Mona Lisas*. He also created 100 silkscreen variations of *The Last Supper*.

The 1969 color lithograph *Color Numerals: Figure 7* by Pop/Abstract Expressionist painter **Jasper Johns** depicts a rainbow-colored Mona with a huge handprint of the artist.

Mary Beth Edelson's *Some Living American Women Artists/Last Supper* (1971) superimposes photographs of modern female artists (like Georgia O'Keeffe, who's masquerading as Jesus) over the heads of the apostles who sit around Leonardo's table.

Gary Larson modeled the bovine creation on the cover of *The Far Side Gallery 3* (1988), the *Mona Lisa Cow*, after our mysterious lady.

In 1990, the French performance artist **Orlan** underwent plastic surgery to look like Mona—or at least, to have her forehead (she wanted the chin of Botticelli's Venus).

The ad campaign for **Gateway Computers** in the late 1990s and early 2000s, "We made her smile," featured photographs of Mona look-alikes.

Duchamp's L.H.O.O.Q.

materials like raw silk and he experimented with different methods of lifting, from strings and pulleys to pedals and harnesses. Some designs looked like a butterfly or dragonfly; another resembled a windmill. Leonardo also experimented with a primitive helicopter design based on an aerial screw; unfortunately, it required immense amounts of human power, as did his design for an ornithopter (an airplane with flapping wings). Leonardo may even have strapped on a pair of feathers and jumped from his studio in Florence to test his flight devices. Still, the only flight design that has proved the test of time is Leonardo's parachute, which British skydiver Adrian Nicholas built and successfully demonstrated in 2000.

Of the thousands of sketches of models Leonardo left as his legacy, some would have worked; many would have failed. Regardless, one man, Carlo Niccolai, has decided to build some of them. Niccolai re-creates Leonardo's designs using 15th-century materials like brass and wood. His models now reside in the Leonardo Museum in Vinci and can also be purchased. Check out Niccolai's Web site www.arca.net/expo/niccolai/chisiamo.htm for details.

GENIUS ANATOMY

Besides wearing the hats of painter, military engineer, and inventor, Leonardo was also a scientist—not an easy line of work in Renaissance Italy. His methods of scientific inquiry were quite advanced, considering the times. He didn't define the scientific method (that credit goes to later scientists Francis Bacon, Galileo Galilei, and Isaac Newton), but he did consider observation to be the best way to understand the natural world. He looked around, asked questions, formulated hypotheses, tested what he could, and then developed theories. Like his inventions, not all of his scientific musings hit the mark, but many anticipated modern theories.

Dabbling in botany, Leonardo designed a garden for Ludovico Sforza in Milan, wrote about the structure of plants, and painted directly from nature—check out the juniper foliage in *Ginevra de' Benci*. Studying geological processes, he theorized correctly about how rivers carve mountains and how water once covered the entire earth. In a rebuke to the Church, he even challenged the Great Flood story by showing the presence of successive strata of fossils in a river basin, which suggested no Great Flood could ever have occurred. Leonardo also studied optics, hydrology, mechanics, and astronomy (sadly, he didn't invent the telescope).

LEO SAYS

"Science is the observation of things possible, whether present or past. Prescience is the knowledge of things which may come to pass, though but slowly."

Leonardo's greatest scientific legacy was his unparalleled anatomical studies. Many of his predecessors, including Alberti, had instructed painters how to draw the body properly, layer by layer, bone by bone. Some anatomists carried out dissection experiments on animals and challenged antiquated medical and anatomical ideas from Aristotle, Galen, and medieval doctors. But Leonardo, who wanted to know how each part of the human body worked, produced hundreds of drawings that formed the basis of modern anatomical illustration.

Unlike many of his colleagues, Leonardo actually dissected human cadavers, although the Church forbade most post-mortem dissections (criminals were generally considered suitable subjects for such poking around). Late at night in the crypt of a church that doubled as a morgue, Leonardo explored the inner bowels—literally—of his cadavers, applying his knowledge of machines to the bodies he dissected. Muscles operated similarly to springs, for example. As illustrated in *Vitruvian Man*, Leonardo saw fixed proportions in the human body. This divine relationship linked each body part to the entire person, even if, contrary to Langdon's claim, Leonardo didn't prove that the ratios always equal PHI.

Leonardo drew muscle and bone groups correctly, identifying the heart as a muscle. After comparing the deaths of a young child and an old man, Leonardo recognized arteriosclerosis of the aorta—half a century before anyone else. And, when he pithed a live frog, he discovered the spinal cord as the origin of nerves, or "generative" power. Leonardo, of course, made some mistakes. At first he compared the layering of the human brain to that of an onion, and couldn't quite figure out where the soul resided. And, sex—from female organs to the act itself—seems to have thrown

Did You Know . . . ?

■ Leonardo believed that facial characteristics revealed a person's character. In his grotesque drawing *Old Man with Ivy Wreath and Lion's Head* (c. 1503–4), for instance, the man's leonine features imply bravery.

■ Some historians speculate that Leonardo's mother, Caterina, was Jewish. According to Jewish law, that would mean Leonardo was Jewish too.

■ Leonardo may have been a synesthete—one whose sensory experiences are often mixed messages and as a result can "taste" or "hear" colors or "see" music.

■ Talk about perfectionism: while painting *The Last Supper*, Leonardo would sometimes stare at the wall for hours, make one small brush stroke, then go home.

■ Sigmund Freud claimed that a dream Leonardo had about a kite (a predatory bird) signified his homosexuality. But Freud mistranslated the Italian word *nibbio* ("kite") as "vulture," which was an Egyptian symbol for mother, hence the interpretation that he was repressing love for his mother and other women.

LEONARDO

him for a loop. Nonetheless, Leonardo's detailed, graceful drawings show an extraordinary understanding of human anatomy.

Around 1495, he designed, though likely never built, the world's first mechanical robot—one of Saunière's fascinations in the *Code* (though it doesn't get as much play as the cryptex). Leonardo based his armored robot on the "perfect" proportions of *Vitruvian Man* and designed working parts from head to toe. In line with his comparison of the human body to a complicated machine, Leonardo experimented with three-degrees-of-freedom joints, and wrists with four degrees of freedom. A water- or weight-powered cable powered the humanoid. This robot template, the sum of many parts of the human machine, perfectly bridged Leonardo's anatomical and mechanical studies.

LEARNING MORE ABOUT LEO

For good reason, Leonardo has remained the icon of Renaissance genius for half a millennium. Not only was he a gifted artist, but his all-around thinking put him head and shoulders above his peers. While he built on existing bodies of knowledge, his fertile imagination made leaps and grasped possibilities beyond the ken of his society. Had Leonardo more widely shared his knowledge, inventions, and discoveries during his lifetime, he might have had a tremendous impact on progress in many fields, from mechanics to aeronautics. Instead we must remain content in the knowledge that contemporaries revered him as one of the artistic masters of his day. If you'd like to learn more, here's where to turn:

From the horse's mouth:

Leonardo's Notebooks, edited by H. Anna Suh (Black Dog & Leventhal, 2005). This oversized tome pairs the translation with art reproductions.

The Notebooks of Leonardo da Vinci, edited by Jean Paul Richter (2 volumes, Dover Publications, 1970). Translations of Leonardo's notebooks.

Treatise on Painting by Leonardo da Vinci, translated by John Francis Rigaud (Kessinger, 2004). Various editions of this work record Leonardo's thoughts on painting.

Popular biographies and histories:

Inventing Leonardo by A. Richard Turner (University of California Press, 1992). An examination of Leonardo's legacy over the past four centuries.

Leonardo by Martin Kemp (Oxford University Press, 2004). A fascinating account of Leonardo's life and times, by one of the world's experts.

Leonardo da Vinci: Flights of the Mind by Charles Nicholl (Viking, 2004). A graceful account of Leonardo's inspirations and influences.

Leonardo da Vinci: The Mind of the Renaissance by Alessandro Vezzosi (Gallimard, 1996). A short, stylish, heavily illustrated paperback.

Renaissance overviews:

The Civilization of Europe in the Renaissance by John R. Hale (Scribner, 1994). A decidedly unstuffy approach to daily life at the end of Christendom and the beginnings of modern Europe.

The Italian Renaissance: Culture and Society in Italy by Peter Burke (Princeton University Press, 1999). A social and cultural history of the Italian Renaissance.

The symbolism of the clues meshed too perfectly—the pentacle, *The Vitruvian Man*, Da Vinci, the goddess, and even the Fibonacci sequence. All inextricably tied." —*The Da Vinci Code*

Lefty Leonardo's mirror-image handwriting (right) was likely an attempt to make his words legible, not to obfuscate them.

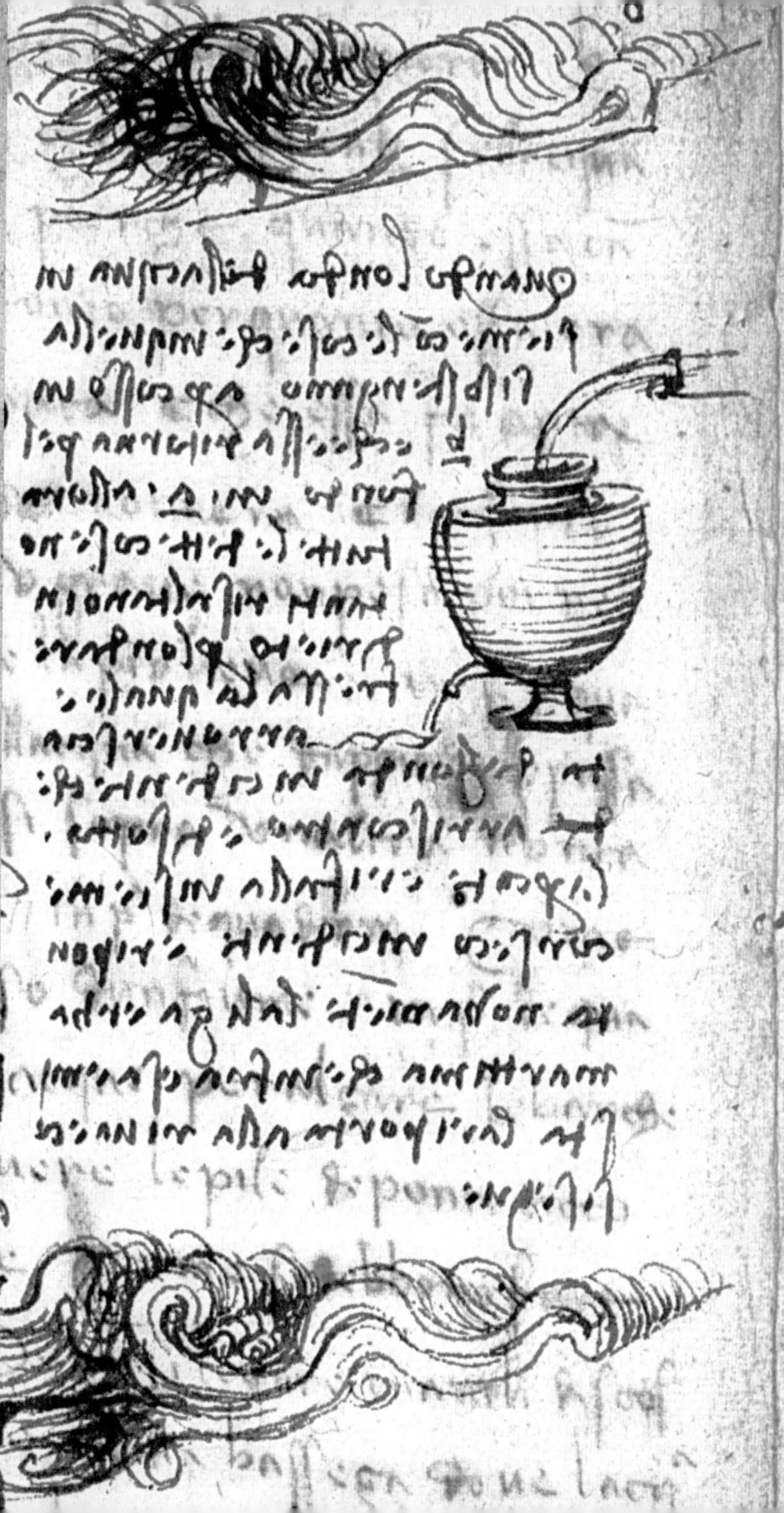

While the Pope's summer retreat, Castel Gandolfo (right), is off-limits to the public, you can delve into the Vatican Museums (below).

ylmere imon bellaci scorem
any emeare bella murlaci terra
no bimisionno diquella

om e iamas parso pla pannabyse
ie va inasto e lo so plctagliaim mi
e somisisacom eleberta glo
omi aleese de mon pla tagliaom boni
e denasto sisua
mi falaca eronni sicbla ploro pi
ure le le some aleese demon

milmere faco largni sllasso malto
benano plosanso plerouin bellesome
iege te ghalnsimmori

sicomi lomom bellataghaim biro
nfacio sansussino vooas
estera solo aleesmodelmo de slose qual
mods: ancom lacon vorsaio
llasse demon impse ese acoro
oln momi simobano

In 2002, Skysport Engineering built a glider based on one of Leonardo's designs for flying machines (left). They pulled off a few successful test flights (right), shown in the documentary "Leonardo's Dream Machines."

Leonardo's scientific work, such as his studies for how light hits a human face (above), informed his painting (Lady with an Ermine, *left*).

rome & the vatican

Opus Dei Pulls Secret Strings

WHEN HE LEARNS THAT AN ages-old secret society is about to make shocking statements about Jesus and Mary Magdalene, Opus Dei Bishop Manuel Aringarosa travels by night to Rome, where he is whisked away by car to Castel Gandolfo. This fortified palace, off-limits to the public, is primarily the Pope's summer retreat.

BEHIND THE WALLS OF VATICAN CITY

Ever wonder which is the smallest country in the world? You may have been there without knowing it. In fact, if you've ever been to Rome and visited St. Peter's Basilica or browsed the Vatican Museums, you have. The Vatican, at .2 square miles or .44 square kilometers, is not only the seat of world Catholicism, it's also the world's smallest nation. Curious about how it came to be in the heart of the Eternal City and what goes on behind those guarded walls? Read on.

Although the institution to which it owes its existence is more than 2,000 years old, the State of the Vatican City, as it is formally known, is actually very young. It is even younger than Italy, which officially appeared on the map in 1861 and included among its constituent parts a large chunk of territories that the Church had ruled since the Middle Ages.

Rome was not initially part of the new Italy. In fact, Rome and a portion of the surrounding region, a much-reduced remnant of the Church's former dominions, remained under papal rule until 1870. Then, during the Franco-Prussian War, Italian troops entered the city and overcame the feeble resistance of the papal army, making Rome the capital of Italy the following year.

Pope Pius IX, however, refused to recognize the newly unified country. For the next 59 years, he and his successors lived as self-proclaimed prisoners in the Vatican, never setting foot outside its walls. Only in 1929 did the pope formally recognize Italy's sovereignty over the territories of the former Papal States. Italy, in turn, recognized the independence of the Vatican enclave in the center of Rome.

And so Vatican City, consisting of St. Peter's Basilica plus 108 acres of gardens and palaces, joined the roster of nations. Beyond the walls, several additional buildings have extraterritorial status, among them the major basilicas of San Giovanni and Santa Maria Maggiore, the Lateran Palace, and the pope's summer palace at Castel Gandolfo.

This ain't just real estate. When UNESCO placed Vatican City on the World Heritage List in 1984, it cited a long list of priceless treasures: the works of Renaissance and baroque architects Bramante and Bernini; Michelangelo's ceiling in the Sistine Chapel; Raphael's Stanza della Segnatura frescoes, and more.

In terms of government, this pint-sized nation is a rarity—a non-hereditary, elective monarchy, with full legislative, executive, and judicial powers vested in the pope, who is the chief of state of Vatican City and supreme authority of the Holy See, the central government of the Roman Catholic Church.

The spiritual home of more than a billion Catholics worldwide, Vatican City has a population of approximately 500 residents, mainly clergy plus 110 Swiss Guards and other lay persons. Like any other country, the Vatican issues its own currency, the Vatican euro, and has its own bank, called the Institute for Religious Works (IOR—its name in Italian is the *Istituto per le Opere di Religione*). The tiny country issues its own postage stamps and has its own (very efficient) post office. It has its own phone system, an

ROME & THE VATICAN

electricity-generating plant, a heliport, and a train station, used mostly for freight deliveries.

Vatican City also has its own media. Its newspaper, *L'Osservatore Romano,* comes out daily in Italian, weekly in several other languages. The radio station, Radio Vaticana, broadcasts daily in 30-plus languages and invites you to tune in "for Heaven's sake." Satellite TV channels, check; publishing house, check; Web site, check (www.vatican.va).

Running both the Church and the state involves more than 4,000 Vatican employees, and a major perk of working there is shopping there. The Vatican pharmacy, run by brothers of the Fatebenefratelli order since 1874, is open to anyone with a doctor's prescription. Not so the cherished Vatican supermarket, Anona, which can only be used by those who hold a *tessera,* or pass. If you've got one, you can indulge in an impressive variety of foods, beverages, and tobaccos from around the world, all of it tax-free. The tessera is also required to shop at the Vatican City department store, Supermercato Tessuti, set in the train station. This is where Vatican fashionistas go for high-end clothes, also tax-free.

The Vatican City State is defended by the Swiss Guard, which has been the pope's private security force since 1506. Only Roman Catholic males of Swiss nationality and good moral character may join this prestigious military corps. Recruits must be between 19 and 30, at least 5'8" tall, and unmarried (they may later marry), and they must have completed basic training in the Swiss army. They wear a dress uniform of red, blue, and gold stripes often said to have been designed by Michelangelo (the ultimate in designer duds, if it were true!) and carry concealed modern firearms in addition to the sixteenth century–style halberd.

One of the duties of the Swiss Guard is to defend the entrances to Vatican City, so don't expect to push deep into this foreign land. The only way to penetrate farther than St. Peter's Basilica, the Vatican Museums, or the Paul VI Audience Hall is to take the guided tour of the Vatican gardens offered at 10 a.m. on Saturday year-round (also Tuesday and Thursday from March through October). Unfortunately, there is no straying off the beaten path. Nor will anyone stamp your passport.

CASTEL GANDOLFO: THE POPE'S SUMMER CAMP

Although Bishop Aringarosa sees Castel Gandolfo as a gloomy, forbidding place, the town usually gives visitors a cheerful first impression. Perched high above scenic Lake Albano, on the crest of an elongated hilltop, it's one of a cluster of lovely villages collectively called the Castelli Romani, or "Roman castles."

Located about 20 miles southeast of Rome and surrounded by the olive groves and vineyards of Lazio, the village of fewer than 8,000 residents is best known as the Vatican's summer camp. It has served as the annual getaway for popes since the time of Urban VIII (1623–1644). Because of its small-town vibe, Castel Gandolfo is an intimate setting for the Sunday morning papal blessings in the town's small piazza, which is right outside the front door of the Palazzo Pontificio (Papal Palace). The palace is technically part of the Vatican, not Italy. Unfortunately, you won't be able to cross international borders on a visit here—the Holy Father's retreat is not open to the public.

The Papal Palace is a much mellower holy site than St. Peter's Basilica in Rome. The inviting, five-tiered palace, with its stately ocher façade and carriage ramp sloping up from the piazza, presents a welcome backdrop to the main square. The visiting faithful and curious tourists throng the piazza, hitting the T-shirt shops and *gelaterie* (ice cream parlors).

Designed by Carlo Maderno, a key figure in the architectural transition from Renaissance to baroque, the Papal Palace was built in 1624 on the ruins of a 12th-century fortification.

Atop the palace sit the slightly incongruous beanie-shaped domes of the observatory. The twin-domed Specula Vaticana, characterized in the novel as a symbol of conflict between church and science, is indeed within the Papal Palace. It was founded in 1935 by a group of astronomer-Jesuits who found stargazing easier in Castel Gandolfo than in Rome, where city lights obscured the sky.

Although the telescopes and other equipment from the observatory have been moved to a facility in Tucson, Arizona, the Papal Palace still contains a museum with antique telescopes and meteorites, as well as an extensive library of rare books on astronomy.

ROME & THE VATICAN

(Alas, both the museum and library are off-limits to all but serious students of astronomy.) It's ironic that the Papal Palace should be home to these activities, given that the Inquisition once condemned Galileo for insisting that the earth revolves around the sun.

In front of the palace, on the Piazza della Libertà, sits a small jewel: the church of San Tommaso di Villanova (1659). Designed by Maderno's student, the baroque sculptor and architect Gianlorenzo Bernini (who also designed the town's square), the church's streaked red exterior gives the façade a rusted look. The interior is a marvel of baroque understatement—a neat trick from a master architect who could make history's busiest period look restrained. A painting of the Crucifixion behind the altar shows Mary Magdalene at Jesus' feet.

> **L E O S A Y S**
>
> "What is spiritual in us is made of the power of the imagination . . ."

Setting out from the main square and walking along the crest of the hill, you can cover the entire distance between the Papal Palace and the papal gardens in a short stroll. The main street, Corso della Repubblica, is lined with small businesses like Angela's fresh ravioli store and several barber shops. On a parallel road, Via dei Zecchini, a bit down the slope on the lake side, you'll find two restaurants with fine views of the countryside and Lake Albano. Hotel Bucci, on the alley of Santa Lucia Filippini, includes an arbor-covered outdoor *ristorante*. The Taverna del Cacciatore dishes up *la cucina romana* accompanied by wines from nearby towns, like San Tommaso's Giano Lazio, or a Frascati from Gotto D'oro. Menu prices in Castel Gandolfo are a fraction of those in Rome's restaurants.

Down the hill and walled off from view are the papal gardens, which are entered through another elegant palazzo, that of the Barberini family, to which Pope Urban VIII belonged. (The carved stone bees that decorate the façade are the symbol of the Barberini dynasty.) The splendid descriptions of the gardens found in coffee-table art books are only a tease, as the public is not allowed to enter the grounds.

The formal landscaping spreads down the hillside away from the lake for several hundred acres. Because the hilltop location attracts whatever breezes may blow through Lazio even on the hottest summer day, this has been a choice rural location for Roman VIPs dating back to the time of Emperor Domitian, who

Famous & Infamous Popes

*A*s Mel Brooks once said, "It's good to be the king." Well, the same goes for popes—but you don't have to *be* good to be the pope. Among the 264 past popes, here are some of the most, well, colorful characters.

■ **She-Pope:** Pope Joan, 9th century. According to one version of this legend, an Englishwoman posing as a man was elected Pope John VIII in 855 and served for just over two years. Her sex was supposedly discovered when she gave birth to a child during a papal procession, prompting a mob to stone both her and the baby to death.

■ **Precociously Debauched:** John XII (955–963), Roman. The reign of young John XII, elected between 16 and 18 years of age, was notorious for his debauchery, incest (his niece, sisters, and his mother, it's said!), and poor political decisions. He eventually died *in coitus.*

■ **Patron of the Arts:** Sixtus IV (1471–84), Francesco della Rovere, Italian. Built the Sistine Chapel and commissioned artists such as Perugino and Botticelli to fresco its walls.

■ **Most Notorious:** Alexander VI (1492–1503), Rodrigo de Borgia, Spanish. His life was a nonstop frenzy of greed, nepotism, incest, and murder. At least one of his seven children was a chip off the old block: Cesare Borgia was the prototype for Machiavelli's famous prince.

■ **The Warrior:** Julius II (1503–13), Giuliano della Rovere, Italian. To secure territories for the Papal States, the "warrior pope" sent armies throughout Italy. He also commissioned Michelangelo to paint the Sistine Chapel ceiling.

■ **Bullheaded:** Leo X (1513–21), Giovanni de' Medici, Italian. A lover of the finer things, he ran the Vatican into the red rebuilding St. Peter's Basilica. To refill the coffers, he granted a bull of indulgence, allowing the faithful to buy an entry pass into Heaven. In response, Martin Luther wrote his 95 Theses, launching the Protestant Reformation.

■ **The Immovable Force:** Paul V (1605–21), Camillo Borghese, Italian. Famous for having censured the discoveries of Galileo. (See Dan Brown's *Angels & Demons.*)

■ **Mr. Right:** Pius IX (1846–78), Giovanni Maria Mastai-Ferretti, Italian. His bull *Ineffabilis*, declaring the Virgin Mary "exempt from all stain of original sin," proclaimed the Immaculate Conception as Church dogma. He also convened the First Vatican Council, which defined the dogma of papal infallibility.

ROME & THE VATICAN

built a palace on the plot of ground now occupied by the papal gardens.

Visiting Castel Gandolfo

A perfect time to visit Castel Gandolfo is the first Sunday in September, when the summer heat starts to dissipate and the town celebrates St. Sebastian, its patron, with a festival that includes fireworks over Lake Albano. There is also a peach festival the last Sunday of July, when the nearby orchards are laden with the fruit.

Trains leave Rome's Stazione Termini every hour for the 40-minute journey to Albano. The Castel Gandolfo station is not well marked, so keep an eye out for it after you spot the town (look for the domes of the church and the observatory) in the distance. From the station, it's a steep climb up a switchback road, appropriately called via della Stazione, into town.

london & roslin

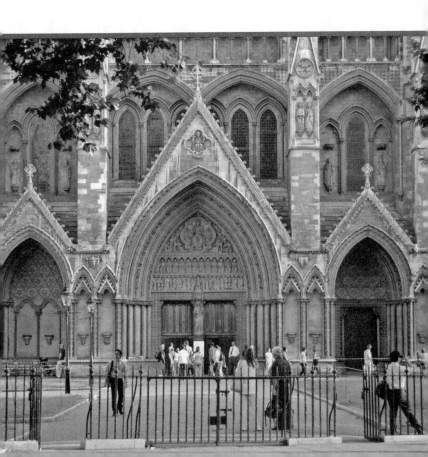

Dead End

SAFELY ABOARD TEABING'S PRIVATE JET, Sophie, Langdon, and Teabing find another clue. Landing in London, the threesome hastily interpret the latest lead and make a mad dash down Fleet Street, the street made infamous by its pubs and the press, to a Templar church. The 12th-century church exudes medieval mystique, thanks to the incredibly lifelike effigies of nearly a dozen Templar knights.

FLEET STREET'S GORE, GRIME & GUINNESS

Fleet Street is the main route between the City, London's financial center, and Westminster, the heart of royal and political clout. But the street is more than a conduit between seats of power—it has power of its own, too. This was once the hub of London's newspaper trade (*see* the Street of Shame sidebar *below*), a virtual village of scoops and scandals. Its deep-rooted, vivid history made the name Fleet Street synonymous with the British press.

The first newspaper here, the *Daily Courant*, opened for business in 1702, and other newspapers steadily gravitated to the area. *The Times,* which started life as the *Daily Universal Register*, set up shop in 1785 and the *Daily Telegraph* entered the ring in 1855. In 1900 the *Daily Express* was established at 121–128 Fleet Street; its distinctive black-and-chrome art-deco building, dubbed the Black

Street of Shame

$\int$ leet Street has been called the "Street of Shame" for centuries, but not because of the prostitutes who once loitered here. The nickname refers to London's sometimes scandal-besotted publishing trade, which began in 1500 when printer Wynkyn de Worde set up a printing press on Fleet Street, in the shadow of St. Paul's Cathedral and the law courts of the Chancery.

Although publishing in the 1500s was limited to religious tomes and the occasional broadside trumpeting news of natural disasters and malformed births, Fleet Street by the 1720s was home to at least two dozen "newssheets," including the *Daily Courant*. Location is everything and London's emerging press corps certainly knew the value of their address. Being near St. Paul's and the law courts put publishers close to the action, but it also meant the Crown knew where to go when it chose to crack down on free speech, which it did with astonishing regularity until the mid-1700s (usually by raising taxes on paper).

Fudging the truth was common among Fleet Street's earliest wordsmiths, and the ease with which editorial opinions could be bought here resulted in that "Street of Shame" nickname. Shame thickened in the late 1800s, when Fleet Street editors began a fierce competition for dwindling readers (sound familiar?). "If it bleeds it leads" might as well have been the reigning mantra as erstwhile editorialists suddenly found themselves working the murder beat. Even icons of integrity like the *London Times* got in on the act, which reached its gory apex with the Jack the Ripper murders of the 1880s.

Fleet Street was no less bloodthirsty in the 20th century, though scandal replaced gore at the newsstand. From the John Profumo affair of the 1960s to the salacious coverage of Chuck and Di, scandal-mongering kept Fleet Street's writers in pints. All the rubbernecking became an irritant to England's gilded class, however, and in the early 1980s the Home Office began investigating abuses of freedom, declaring that "Fleet Street had a year to clean up its act." It did better than that. By the late 1980s, the onset of digital media had decentralized publishing, and most of the newspapers on Fleet Street decamped to Wapping in search of cheaper rent. Today, only the pubs remain, a yeasty testament to a florid past.

LONDON & ROSLIN

Lubyanka, was designed in 1931 by Ellis and Clarke. Across the street, at number 85, you can see the stone Reuters building (1935), designed by Sir Edwin Lutyens.

By the time Langdon and the other Grail chasers passed these monuments to the publishing trade on their way to Temple Church, such buildings were merely reminders of Fleet Street's pulpy past. In 1986, Rupert Murdoch, owner of *The Times*, the *Sunday Times* and *The Sun*, introduced digital technology that replaced the typesetters and machine workers, cutting production costs and ending the unions' power to stop the presses in one fell swoop. Massive layoffs of print workers and journalists resulted in a violent, year-long strike. Murdoch's move paved the exit route for other Fleet Street newspapers, most of which left during the 1980s. Financial companies, such as Goldman Sachs (in the *Daily Telegraph*'s old home), are the new residents here.

The quiet conversations of investment bankers are a far cry from the "read all about it!" yells of Fleet Street's glory days, when typesetting equipment and presses roared through the night. **Both work and social life flowed on a river of alcohol, and editors were more likely to find their staff in a pub than at their desks.** One pub even had a bell warning reporters to dash back to the newsroom. (For details on places where you can still bend your elbow, *see* the Bottoms Up sidebar *below*.)

These days, trendy bars and chain stores run neck and neck with the pubs, and fancy coffees rather than pints of beer are the drink of choice. Though the reputation for action and scandal-mongering lingers, let's face it: Fleet Street today looks a lot like an average business district. Now it's up to *The Beano*, a classic kids' comic still published at 185 Fleet Street, to provide a flicker of that old feisty spirit.

Beyond the pubs and papers, the street is also known for St. Bride's, known as the journalists' church. Its prominent, soaring spire, designed by Sir Christopher Wren in 1703, is the tallest of his steeples. (Legend has it that this shape inspired the tiered form of wedding cakes.) Samuel Pepys and other greats of the press are buried in the crypt, now a museum charting the church's rich religious and inky history. When the last major news company, Reuters, left Fleet Street in June 2005, a ceremonial send-off service was fittingly held in this church.

Bottoms Up

hen in London and the subject turns to pubs, you'll find there's no shortage of canteens in which to wet your whistle, especially in the Fleet Street area. Here are a few of the best.

El Vino. A popular lunch spot for besuited sixtysomethings, El Vino's main draw is its impressive range of wines. Cynical attorneys carry on the backslapping chit-chat that is unlikely to have changed since this wine bar opened for business in 1879. ✉ *47 Fleet Street, 020/7353–5384.* Ⓤ *Blackfriars.*

The Old Bank of England. One of the capital's most gloriously decorated drinking venues has dizzily high ceilings, chandeliers, and an island bar so tall it might render your drink unreachable. There's something exciting about throwing back your pint of ale and thinning your wallet while knowing you're in an 1888 building that once housed the Bank of England. You can also get a generous helping of pie here, but think twice—this building was built on the site where demon barber Sweeney Todd was believed to have butchered his clients and turned them into meat pies. ✉ *194 Fleet Street, 020/7430–2255.* Ⓤ *Temple.*

The Punch Tavern. Themed on Punch & Judy puppet shows, this 1897 watering hole is where writers came to drink up and think up the satirical magazine *Punch*. The interior is ornate, with an etched skylight and period furniture. It's become a trendy destination among Fleet Street pubs, with a buffet and menu that cater to businessfolk. ✉ *99 Fleet Street, 020/7353–6658.* Ⓤ *Blackfriars.*

The Tipperary. The oldest Irish pub in London was also the world's first pub outside Ireland to serve Guinness; punters have been draining the stout here since 1794. The music and the design may be more up-to-date these days, but the vibe still harks back to Fleet Street's glory days, when blue pencils and printers rubbed inkstained elbows along the narrow bar. ✉ *66 Fleet Street, 020/7583–6470.* Ⓤ *Temple.*

Ye Olde Cheshire Cheese. Established in 1667, Ye Olde Cheshire Cheese feels remarkably in touch with its 17th-century past. Tourists and Londoners alike lurk here, finding a seat along the bare benches built into dark brown walls. The Cellar Bar, a furtive seating area down a flight of stone steps, invites conspiracy among those crouched over a serious pint of lager and a lamb chop. ✉ *145 Fleet Street, 020/7353–6170.* Ⓤ *Blackfriars.*

LONDON & ROSLIN

But the past isn't completely dead here. In Wren's day, Fleet Street's reputation for rot wasn't solely the result of its scandal-obsessed journalists. Rottenness also emanated from the sewage-choked Fleet River, which once flowed here. Wren engineered the river into a canal, and in 1766 the river was channeled underground. If you stand by a manhole cover at the eastern end of Fleet Street, and if the traffic isn't too loud, you'll hear the Fleet River flowing by in the sewer—a true echo from the past.

TEMPLE CHURCH

London's Temple Church, on Inner Temple Lane, may be the oldest Gothic church in Britain. Teabing describes it as an "Eerie old place . . . pagan to the core," but there's nothing dark or shadowy about this bright and airy building faced with golden Caen stone. It's also directly connected to the most Christian of all Christian churches: the Church of the Holy Sepulchre in Jerusalem. There's no question, though, that it has a magical atmosphere.

Wherever they established Temples, the Knights Templar built round churches to remind themselves of the dome raised over the site of the burial and resurrection of Jesus. This one, built in the center of the New Temple lands, was consecrated in 1185 by Heraclius, Patriarch of Jerusalem. Its original nave (sometimes also called the choir or the chancel) was built on a small scale, to balance the round church. But King Henry III (1216–1272) rather fancied being buried among the Templars so a new, grander nave was built and consecrated in 1240. Later, the king's will revealed he had changed his mind, choosing Westminster Abbey for his burial instead.

During the Crusades in the 12th and 13th centuries, the round church was not simply a reminder of Jerusalem; Templar clerics taught that it *was* Jerusalem, an idea widely believed by all knights. Being buried in the Temple Church was, to the medieval knight, the same as being buried in consecrated ground in Jerusalem. There, on Judgment Day, the Last Trump would be sounded, summoning God's warriors into battle with the forces of

Satan. This probably explains the appearance of the most striking elements of the round church: the knights' effigies.

They are figures of men in their prime, alert and ready, eyes wide open. Their swords are drawn as if ready for battle. The crossed legs of a few of the knights suggest, in the iconography of the time, that the recumbent figures are walking toward the viewer.

Today Temple Church serves the two societies of The Temple: the Inner and Middle Temples. It is one of a handful of English churches that enjoys the status of Royal Peculiar, meaning its clergymen are appointed by the Queen herself. The church is helmed by the Master of the Temple. In the 13th century, a man in this position was a Baron of the Realm, controlling so many lands and estates that he outranked all other ambassadors and peers at church councils. The current Reverend and Valiant Master of the Temple, Robin Griffith-Jones, is a mild and likeable man who tells people that he is master of nothing. "Sadly, I inherited only the title."

Sadly too, we have inherited very little of the original church. Almost from its beginning, people have been rebuilding it. Some of the exterior north wall is of original, rough stone construction and the great West Door, surrounded by carved Norman arches, dates from 1185. But the rest of the building is a pastiche of later changes.

The church escaped damage in the Great Fire of London (1666). Sir Christopher Wren, charged with rebuilding dozens of other churches, couldn't keep his hands off it anyway (*see* the Master Builder sidebar *below*). The unusual text-decorated *reredos* or altar screen, at the eastern end of the nave, is his design.

Even the knights' effigies have been tampered with—in their case, by 19th-century fixer-uppers. The effigies were put in their current positions during a Victorian restoration in 1841. Now they lie five on the south side, on your left upon entering the church, and five on the north side. Seven tombs found during that restoration, under the floor of the round church, are thought to be connected with some of the effigies.

The group on the right includes four knights and the mysterious closed casket described in the novel; there seems to be no explanation for the casket. These four knights were damaged almost

TEMPLE CHURCH

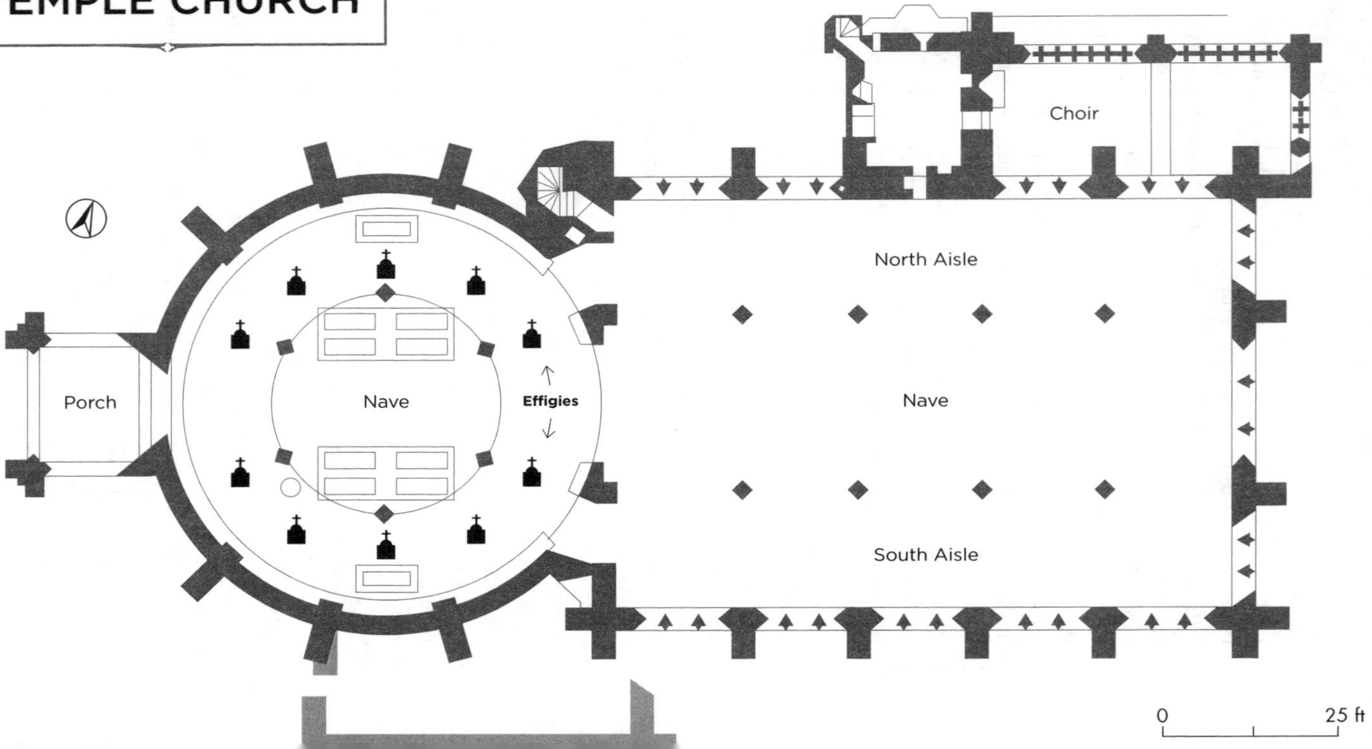

Porch

Nave

Effigies

Nave

North Aisle

South Aisle

Choir

0   25 ft

beyond recognition during WWII. On May 10, 1941 at the height of the Luftwaffe's air raids on London, incendiary bombs set fire to the church roof, ultimately burning all the woodwork in the church. A painting near the south portico shows the effigies covered in molten lead from the burning roof. The work is by Kathleen Allen, who painted the destruction the morning after the raid.

The group of knights on the left, facing the west door, are less damaged than the knights on the right, retaining most of their original, highly stylized features.

Temple Church is known for more than its effigies. A scattering of markers detail its other milestones, like the plaque under the organ pipes that commemorates Richard Hooker, Master of the Temple in 1585. In a historic series of pulpit debates with his deputy Walter Travers, who was a Calvinist, he defined Anglican theology. Today he is known as the father of Anglicanism. Not every milestone is theological, though. How many churches can you name that have a connection to "Top of the Pops"? One of the first classical records to sell a million copies, Mendelssohn's *O For the Wings of a Dove,* was recorded here in 1927.

Visiting Temple Church

Temple Church is open weekdays between 11 a.m. and 4 p.m. and all day Sunday. It's often closed for private functions; check the schedules posted on the church's Web site (www.templechurch. com). For more information, call 020/7353–3470.

ЗAND OF TEMPLAR BROTHERS

One of the engines that drives *The Da Vinci Code,* the mystery at its heart, is the secret of the Templars. As Langdon tells Sophie, the Templars found something in the ruins of Solomon's Temple in Jerusalem, "something that made them wealthy and powerful beyond anyone's wildest imagination." The novel goes on to suggest that the secret concerned the true nature of the Holy Grail. Actually, the Templars *did* have a secret and, for a relatively short time, it made them astonishingly wealthy and powerful.

Master Builder

$\mathcal{A}$ small, frail child who liked drawing and science, the young Christopher Wren would be described today as a bit of a bookworm. Wren was born in Wiltshire, England, in 1632. He grew up in a rarefied academic environment and the son of Charles I was a regular playmate—a connection that was to serve Wren well. He started his professional life as an astronomy professor, but it was architecture, not stargazing, that was to make his reputation.

Wren's love of classic design, geometry, and astronomy strongly influenced his architectural work. He first won notice with the jewel-like Sheldonian Theatre in Oxford (1664). In 1666, the Great Fire swept through London, destroying nearly a hundred churches and thousands of houses. Wren's former playmate, the extravagant Charles II, seized the opportunity to redesign the cityscape. Within days after the fire, Wren knocked together a proposal to replace the old narrow streets packed with wooden buildings with wide streets lined with brick and stone buildings. Though Charles II didn't embrace the whole plan, he did appoint Wren to be one of the commissioners in charge of rebuilding the city.

The task was mammoth, including no fewer than 51 churches. For churches like St. Bride's, Wren developed his signature tiered spire design. St. Paul's Cathedral, where work began in 1669 and continued for 35 years, is considered Wren's greatest achievement. It has the third largest dome in the world—which wasn't in the officially approved plan, but luckily Wren found his loopholes. He pulled off the feat by building two domes, with a lower interior dome connected to the exterior shell by a structural cone.

Happily, Wren saw St. Paul's completed; he lived to the ripe old age of 91. Wren's tomb in the cathedral bears the Latin epitaph "Reader, if you seek his monument, look around you." By the way, if you're wondering what inspired Teabing to have Sophie and Langdon impersonate "Mr. and Mrs. Christopher Wren the Fourth," this was nothing more than a masterly piece of subterfuge on Teabing's part. The last of the male line of Wrens died out in the early 1900s. Wren's only professional connection to the Temple Church was some restoration work in the late 17th century, later undone in the 19th century. Quick thinking, Teabing . . . .

The Starting Gate

The Poor Knights of Christ and the Temple of Solomon, as the Templars were officially known, were established in Jerusalem in 1118, after the First Crusade. Founded by a Norman knight, Hugh de Payens, and eight other crusader companions, they were Christendom's first military-religious order. They pledged to defend the Temple and the city, to guard the holy shrines, to shelter visitors and, in the words of 17th-century chronicler Father Hay, "to guard them safely throughout the Holy Land to view such things as there were to be seen."

Henry I, Norman King of England, dispatched de Payens in 1128 to recruit English and Scottish knights. Once recruited, knights didn't hang around; they departed for Palestine immediately. So the first London headquarters, near Holborn, was small. (Parts of the foundation of this first center, which became known as the Old Temple, were uncovered as recently as 2002.) But the mission of these mounted and armored Holy Land tour guides captured the imagination of the era's great and good. Soon popes, kings, bishops, and noblemen were throwing money and privileges at them.

By 1186, when the New Temple (a big chunk of riverside London with Temple Church at its center) was consecrated, the Templars' power and wealth in Britain alone was breathtaking. That year, a superior named Geoffrey (also known as a Grand Preceptor or a Master) surveyed their property in England, Scotland, and Ireland, and produced a long list of manors, farms, churches, villages, hamlets, windmills, water mills, rights of common (grazing lands), free warren (the right to hunt game), and advowsons (the right to appoint clerics and to run holy orders).

The Templars were exempt from taxes, fines, and most feudal obligations such as local military service. They were free from tolls at all markets, fairs, bridges, and highways in the kingdom. Within their own manors they could hold courts, impose and levy fines, judge and punish criminals, and confiscate the property of all felons and fugitives.

No one but the king or the chief justice could sue Templars or force them before a court of law. Most importantly, in terms of their powerful secret, all their buildings had the privilege of sanctuary, a medieval law normally reserved to consecrated churches.

LONDON & ROSLIN

If a fugitive claimed sanctuary at the altar of a church, the forces of the law could not pursue him there.

Even some of the Templars' tenants, those permitted to live under the protection of their banner, could share in the exemptions and privileges. Jealous outsiders would sometimes raise the Templar standard, a red cross on a field of white, to try to claim its protections. As long as the loose coalition of crusader knights and nobles held onto Jerusalem, the Templars, as protectors of the holy sites, enjoyed power and prestige throughout Christendom.

Trouble with the Neighbors

Laden with privilege and commanding a quiet, enclosed manor in the middle of crowded and noisy London, it wasn't long before the Templars were getting up people's noses—literally.

Early in his reign, "for the good of his soul and the welfare of the Kingdom," King Henry II (1154–1189) had granted them land on the River Fleet, along with "the whole current of that River," to build a mill. The Fleet, today London's largest subterranean river, once joined the Thames near Blackfriars Bridge. The Templars diverted so much water from the Fleet for their open forges and corn and fulling mills that the river became a stagnant, stinking swamp. In 1290, the prior of the White Friars petitioned the king and Parliament to put an end to "the putrid exhalations arising from the Fleet River which were so powerful as to overcome all the frankincense burnt at their altar during divine service and had occasioned the death of many brethren." The Black Friars, the Bishop of Salisbury, and the Earl of Lincoln all complained that the Templars had diverted the water to their mills and that boats could no longer navigate the Fleet.

The English Templars weren't just nuisance neighbors; they made powerful enemies too. Richard de Hastings, a Grand Preceptor, outraged the king of France when, in 1160, he was entrusted with the dowry of the French Princess Margaret. Margaret and her betrothed, Prince Henry of England, were children. The Templars were meant to protect her dowry—several strategically important French fortresses—until the children were old enough to consummate their marriage. But, as soon as the marriage contracts were signed and the rituals completed, de Hastings handed the fortresses over to the English King Henry II.

The Templar Secret

Such a cavalier attitude toward people in high places is never the smartest way to behave. But for most of their short history the Templars were protected by an elegantly simple secret. They perfected a method of transferring money among themselves using paper.

Traveling Templars needed money to get to the Holy Land and to support themselves once they got there, but crossing continents with valuables was an invitation to highwaymen and thieves. As one of the first international organizations, the English Templars maintained Temples and chapter houses all over Europe and along the Crusaders' routes to Palestine. They devised a system of letters of credit and bills of exchange so that a Templar's valuables deposited in one Temple could be withdrawn in the form of equivalent valuables from another. **At a time when very few people could read and the transmission of information was lengthy and uncertain, this system of written transactions was a breakthrough.** And having a network so trustworthy and extensive gave the Templars tremendous power. In creating this method of exchange for their own use, the Templars joined two other 13th-century groups with international business interests: Genoese merchants and Jews. Many historians credit these three groups with inventing the mechanisms of international banking. Teabing wasn't totally off-base when he called the Templars "the original ATMs."

Norman kings, with estates on both sides of the English Channel, quickly recognized the benefits of these transactions. Nobles, bishops, and rich merchants followed suit, lodging valuables and money in Templar houses. The Temple in London became a storehouse of deposited treasure. The order issued international credit notes, delivered money, paid ransoms, collected taxes and royal revenues, and maintained safe depositories. Eventually, they also loaned money to Christian knights and monarchs.

For a while, widely respected rules of sanctuary protected the Templars and the valuables of their clients. One story tells of Herbert de Burgh, the Earl of Kent, who deposited his riches with the Temple in London. Burgh fell out of favor at court and, after he

LONDON & ROSLIN

was sent to the Tower, the king tried to confiscate his goods. The Templars replied that money entrusted to them "would be delivered to no man without the permission of him who had entrusted it to be kept in the Temple." The Templars may have had custody of the valuables, but the king had custody of de Burgh. Royal torturers prised the requisite permission out of the earl. Until the permission was granted, though, the Templars held firm, as discreet as Swiss bankers.

The End of the Templars

Templar power, virtually unchecked by church or sovereign lords, couldn't last forever. The last crusader stronghold fell in 1291, less than 50 years after the chancel of the London Temple Church was consecrated. The Templars were no longer needed to guard the holy sites. Their new roles as banker and creditor to most of the crowned heads of Europe was a politically dangerous one. Handling so much money made them vulnerable to accusations of corruption and greed. During their glory days, they had cultivated few friends and, in their arrogance, made many enemies. When rumors about their secret rituals and abuses began to spread, no one—except the Pope—stepped forward to save them.

The end of the Templars was instigated by Philip IV of France, also known as Philip the Fair, who was probably a debtor. On October 13, 1307, soldiers of King Philip, operating on secret orders, spread across France and arrested all the Templars at once. One hundred and four wildly fantastic charges were brought against the French Templars. They were accused of secrecy, idolatry, sodomy, and heresy, of spitting and trampling on the cross during initiation rituals, of denying Christ, and of failing to give charity or hospitality. The Master was accused of kissing initiates in intimate and inappropriate places.

Most Templar scholars suggest that the charges were largely untrue. Confessions were obtained through torture so severe that many died of it. Philip the Fair was particularly known for manipulating religious fervor for political ends. It is probably true that the Templars had some kind of secret initiation and systems of passwords to protect their financial transactions, but on this subject history and myth are almost impossible to separate.

Rather than being an active participant in the violent proceedings, as suggested in *The Da Vinci Code*, Pope Clement V (sitting in

Q&A with a Templar Knight

*B*ob Currie is a member of the Masonic Knights Templar and maintainer of the Rosslyn Templars Web site (www. rosslyntemplars.org.uk). He stresses that he speaks only on a personal basis.

Q: After the order was virtually wiped out in the early 14th century, how did it resurrect itself?

A: In 1737 Freemason Andrew Ramsay gave a speech at a Freemason gathering in Paris. He claimed that the Freemasons evolved from the historical crusading knights that fought in the holy land. Ramsay didn't mention any particular order of crusaders, but many Freemasons decided it had to be the Templars. Soon after, numerous Templar orders began to spring up. The earliest record we have of a modern Masonic Knights Templar ritual was a 1769 initiation held in Boston, Massachusetts.

Q: What is expected of a modern knight?

A: A Templar within my tradition, as with all orders in Freemasonry, is expected to abide by the laws of the land and try to assist those in need. We expect members to be upright members of their community and treat others as they would like to be treated.

Q: What are the most common misconceptions regarding the Templars?

A: Linking them with all the famous holy relics, the Holy Grail, Rosslyn chapel, and so on. There has never been any provable historical connection between the Templars and these ideas, and much of it—if not all—is speculation.

Q: Why did you choose to become a Templar?

A: I've always had a keen interest in Scottish history, and Freemasonry played a large part in the social structure of Scotland, particularly from its association with the Operative Stonemasons (the medieval stonemasons who actually built the great cathedrals and castles). I was also fascinated by the story of the Knights Templar and felt that joining the order would be an interesting, perhaps logical, next step in my Masonic career.

Q: If people want to learn more about the Templars, what books would you recommend?

A: *Dungeon, Fire and Sword: The Knights Templar in the Crusades*, by John J. Robinson; *The Rule of the Templars*, by J. M. Upton-Ward; The *Templars*, by Piers Paul Read; and *The Knights Templar: A New History*, by Helen Nicholson.

Avignon, not Rome) was horrified. He annulled the entire French trial and suspended the powers of the bishops and inquisitors.

But the confessions, even though obtained through torture, could not be withdrawn. Philip continued to lobby among nobles and princes of the Church, at one time parading 72 carefully coached stooges before Pope Clement. Fifty-four Templars who recanted confessions given under torture were burned at the stake in 1314, including Jacques de Molay, the last Grand Master. In all, 120 Templars died in France before Pope Clement dissolved the order by Papal Bull in 1312.

No public burnings or executions were reported outside of France. In England, the Templars faced 74 charges of their own, based on the French charges, but they had a quieter end. They were allowed to join other orders or were pensioned off. Their property was confiscated by the Crown and their romantic story became the stuff of legend.

INNER SANCTUM

Enter The Temple through the medieval gates at 17 Fleet Street and you'll be following in the footsteps of Teabing, Sophie, and Langdon, walking up Inner Temple Lane. Hidden behind ordinary buildings, this quiet, atmospheric district is undiscovered territory for most tourists.

Originally the home of the Knights Templar, The Temple was acquired by the Crown, passed to the Knights Hospitallers of St. John, and eventually, in the mid-14th century, given to the law societies today known as the Inner and Middle Temples, two of modern London's four Inns of Court.

The British practice of lawyers training at inns dates from early Norman times, when only priests practiced law. They lived and trained in monastic communities. As the law became secular, the practice of training at an inn—a combination of college and hostel—persisted. Today in Britain, the legal practice is divided between solicitors, lawyers who give advice outside court, and barristers, advocates who appear in court. While law is now taught at universities, barristers must still finish their training by joining chambers in one of the Inns of Court. In a holdover from the early days, novice barristers must eat a specified number of dinners at their inn.

When the courts are in session, you might spot barristers in long black robes rushing along the Temple's paths. Barristers also traditionally wear wigs, but since the wigs are old and uncomfortable to wear, they usually rip them off as soon as they leave the courtroom.

Within the gaslit precinct of The Temple, the buildings of the Inner and Middle Temples are tightly crowded together. You can distinguish them by their identifying plaques, usually posted near a doorway: Pegasus for the Inner Temple and Agnus Dei for the Middle Temple. Middle Templars include five signers of the Declaration of Independence and seven signers of the U.S. Constitution. Every U.S. ambassador is an honorary member. Famous Inner Templars include Chaucer, Bram Stoker, and Mahatma Gandhi.

Though the buildings reflect many different eras, with large sections of post–WWII construction and reconstruction, the footprint of streets dates from the 14th century and earlier. The courtyards and lanes around Temple Church are as they were in the 11th and 12th centuries.

A Walk Through The Temple

The Fleet Street route taken in the book is the most direct approach through The Temple to Temple Church. But the district's other landmarks are fascinating too. This alternate route will give you a fuller picture of The Temple.

From the Temple Underground station, turn left, go up a few steps, then right into Temple Place. Next turn left again into Milford Lane and you'll see an ornate, wrought-iron gate on your right. Don't worry about the sign that says *Private, No Thoroughfare*. If the gate is open, you are permitted to enter. Cross the parking area and you will be facing Middle Temple Garden. Shakespeare used this garden as the setting for the plucking of the roses—red for Lancaster, white for York—that led to the War of the Roses in *Henry VI, Part One*. From May to October, between 12:30 and 3 p.m., the garden is open to the public.

Turn left at the garden and continue along Garden Court, then up a few steps into Fountain Court. Charles Dickens described this courtyard, with its ancient mulberry tree, in *Martin Chuzzlewit*. Turn right and you'll see the magnificent 16th-century Middle Temple Hall. If not being used for a private function, the hall *may* be open to the public and if you're lucky, the hall porter, Mr. Morrissey, may show you some of the highlights. These include the only double hammer-beam ceiling in London and a table made of a hatch cover from Sir Francis Drake's *Golden Hinde* (the ship in which he circumnavigated the globe). Shakespeare's *Twelfth Night* was first performed here by the Lord Chamberlain's Men, the Bard's own company.

Continue to your right, turning right on Middle Temple Lane then left into Crown Office Row. The Inner Temple Gardens are on your right. In summer, take a break to enjoy the roses and 400-year-old oaks and mulberries.

Inner Temple Hall, a private, post-war building, is opposite the garden gates. Facing the hall with your back to the gardens, take the narrow passage around it to your left into Elm Court. The Knight's Buttery, a small, stone building attached to the western end of Inner Temple Hall, includes the oldest rooms still in use in The Temple. Like the rest of Inner Temple Hall, it is private.

Follow around the Buttery to the left, into the Cloisters and Church Court, facing Temple Church. The arched walkways are actually a modern interpretation of the cloisters destroyed in WWII. Walk through the Cloisters, then along Inner Temple Lane, past the ancient West Doorway of the church. Turn right into the lane between Temple Church and Goldsmith Building. The lane ends at the Master's House. Irish playwright and author Oliver Goldsmith (author of *She Stoops to Conquer* and *The Vicar of Wakefield*) is buried here. His grave is marked by a modest plaque in the ground, engraved with a touching tribute from Samuel Johnson, just outside the railings. Don't confuse Goldsmith's grave with its much grander neighbor, an 18th-century tomb of a man whose reputation didn't have the same staying power.

Come back around Temple Church and leave Church Court through the passage opposite the Cloisters. You are now in King's Bench Walk, a terrace of dark brick buildings housing barristers' chambers that date from 1678. If they look familiar, you've probably seen them in such BBC costume dramas as *Vanity Fair, David Copperfield*, and *Oliver Twist*.

Visiting The Temple

Weekdays, the gates are usually open to the public from about 10 a.m. to 6 p.m. On Sunday, use Tudor Gate on Tudor Street. Groups of six or more can arrange tours of the private areas of the Inner Temple; for information, call 020/7797–8241 two weeks in advance. Tours are £12 per person.

Back on the Trail

THE STORY takes a deadly turn in St. James's Park. Langdon and Sophie head to King's College for help in deciphering the latest clue. After cracking it, they race to Westminster Abbey. There they are lured into the Chapter House, a spectacular octagonal room where the walls and floor crawl with symbols. Langdon and Sophie then travel to Scotland's Rosslyn Chapel.

ST. JAMES'S PARK

Bounded by the palaces of Westminster, St. James's, and Buckingham, St. James's Park is the oldest and most royal of the Royal Parks. There's no obvious grit here other than its chilling *Code* association; it's a graceful, tranquil setting for Rémy's seamlessly engineered murder.

The park's roots, though, are less elegant than you might guess. In medieval times, the land was nothing more than a boggy marsh, home to St. James's Leper Hospital from which the park took its name. In 1532, King Henry VIII, that profligate monarch and keen huntsman, bought the marshland to use as a deer park. He replaced the lepers with royals and the hospital with St.

James's Palace. His daughter, Elizabeth I, carried on the trend for partying and hunting here.

It was not until the early 1600s, under James I, that the swamp was drained and the land improved. The park then became a repository for unusual ambassadorial gifts, like elephants, crocodiles, and waterfowl. While you're unlikely to encounter an elephant in the park today, you can spot dozens of species of birds. Duck Island, one of two islands in the park's lake, is home to more than 30 species of geese, ducks, pelicans, and swans. The pelicans arrived in the late-17th century as a gift from a Russian ambassador. Their descendants today inhale whole fish for an eager audience during daily feedings at 4 p.m.

St. James's Park was transformed again in the late 1600s when Charles II returned from exile in France. Inspired by André Le Nôtre's elegant layout of the gardens at Versailles, Charles set about landscaping his park, adding fashionably formal straight tree-lined avenues, a canal, and lush lawns. He also set aside an alley alongside the park—the Mall (rhymes with shall)—where he could play the French croquet-like game of *paille-maille* or pall mall. While the game fell out of fashion, the Mall remained. Today, that distinctively pink-colored road is the main royal processional route from Buckingham Palace.

The park's last makeover came courtesy of architect John Nash in the 1820s. Nash remodeled Buckingham House to make it a palace, turned the canal into a lake, and replaced the formal gardens with a looser, romantic landscape of winding paths, shrubberies, and floral borders. One of the best times to wander the park's paths is at twilight, when you can see Big Ben and the spires of Westminster Abbey soaring above the trees, beyond the lake.

The Horse Guards Parade, facing St. James's Park, is the site of the famous Trooping the Color, an annual ceremony to commemorate the queen's birthday. Henry VIII used this same area as a tiltyard for festivities and jousting tournaments; many gentlemanly scores were settled by jousting here. But with the Parade's proximity to government offices and the queen's residence, the Royal Parks Police won't look kindly on parking a car here, as Rémy did.

Opus Dei's London HQ

$\mathcal{D}$ eep in the quiet, wealthy Bayswater neighborhood on a small, nondescript lane, Opus Dei's London headquarters fill three rambling brick Victorian buildings, of the type you see everywhere in London. It can be hard to imagine low-key 4–6 Orme Court as the site of something as dramatic as Silas's bloody escape.

The popularity of the *Code* has inundated this headquarters with visitors. A steady stream of tourists wander by and peek cautiously inside, hoping to spot something mysterious. As the group's public relations officer told the London *Times*, "They look up at the windows, hoping to spot Silas. But there are no albinos here, nor monks; no Holy Grail behind the bookshelves."

The curious are welcomed politely inside a hushed, dark, businesslike entrance hall and given a basic rundown on the group's activities. In addition to running gender-separate dormitories for its numeraries (working followers), this branch does charitable work in low-income neighborhoods. When asked about the *Code*'s more sensational assertions, Opus Dei representatives will admit that numeraries do wear a spiked cilice, but only to the point of being uncomfortable, not in pain.

OLD SCHOOL

S tumped by another clue, Langdon urges Sophie to try analyzing it the old-fashioned way: by going to a library. The two hustle over to King's College.

King's College is part of the University of London, a top-notch institution with 19,200 students. The university has several campuses around the capital, including the main one on the Strand. The Religion Department of King's College is in the main Strand building; though Brown notes that the department is near Parliament, it's actually quite a hike from that landmark.

And though there is a Research Institute of Systematic Theology at King's College, it doesn't have an electronic research library with "instant answers to any religious historical question" as described in the *Code*. In the novel, a cheerful librarian—complete with comforting pot of tea—searches a massive religion database, helping Langdon and Sophie find the tomb they're looking for. In real life, researchers would have no such luck. The Institute is really little more than a clutch of academics who meet for weekly chats on divine topics.

There is, however, a research room like the one Langdon describes as an octagonal room with a huge round worktable. The Round Reading Room in the college's Maughan Library is a handsome space, with a showstopping rounded skylight.

Brown's choice of King's College for a setting is interesting, considering how his novel unsettles some of the core beliefs of the Anglican Church. King's College was founded in 1829 mostly to snub the competition, University College London, "the godless college in Gower Street," which did away with entry restrictions on race, creed, and political persuasion. King's, by contrast, was seen as a conservative old school Anglican university.

You can take a self-guided tour of the Strand campus of King's College (at the Fleet Street end of the Strand) between 9 a.m. and 5 p.m. on weekdays. Pick up a map and information on the campus from the main reception desk. If you'd like to visit the Theology and Religious Studies Department of the School of Humanities, you need to make an appointment beforehand by calling 020/7836–5454.

EAR ABBEY

A holy place of pilgrimage for more than a thousand years, Westminster Abbey retains its magnetism, a power that's palpable despite the swarms of tourists. (What with the regular sightseers, history buffs who want to gaze at the place where England's monarchs have been crowned, *Code* devotees, and worshippers, odds are slim to none that you'll find the abbey uncrowded as Langdon and Sophie did.)

At first, the clutter of burial slabs, stones, and statues projecting from almost every wall and corner gives the impression of a stonemason's yard. As you reach the nave, lift your eyes to the columns arching upwards along a thundering aisle. The hum of tourist chatter echoes through the cavernous building, punctuated by announcements requesting minutes of silence or prayers. As the novel notes, wardens wear red robes; vergers, who give guided tours, wear black.

The Evolution of a Magnificent Minster

The origins of Westminster Abbey are tangled in myth. The site may have been established as early as the 7th century, when Saxon kings built a "minster" (a particularly large or important church) here. In the 10th century Benedictine monks established an abbey. In 1020, King Edward (later St. Edward the Confessor) founded a church at the abbey, intending it as his burial place. The church was called Westminster, to differentiate it from St. Paul's, the east minster. It was consecrated in 1065, just before Edward's death in 1066. William of Normandy was crowned at Westminster that year, putting the abbey on the map as the coronation place for English sovereigns.

Come the 13th century, the abbey went into a second rebuilding phase, as Henry III began molding it into a Gothic masterpiece complete with a magnificent shrine for St. Edward. Henry died before the work was completed, and it took another 200 years, until the reign of Henry V, to finish.

The legacy of Gothic architecture—all flying buttresses, pointed arches, and ribbed vaulting—is awesome. The single aisles and long nave with transepts (north and south arms) give proportion to the soaring height of the vault, the highest in England at nearly 102 feet. But even this is surpassed by the Chapel of Henry VII (1485–1509), also known as the Lady Chapel. The ceiling is like a series of pirouetting lace circles; mirrors stationed in the center of the chapel help you ogle the carvings above without craning your neck. The sculpted walls are beautifully rippled with a lineup of 117 statues of saints. Keep an eye open for St. Wilgefort, who was so concerned about protecting her chastity that she prayed to God for help and woke up one morning with a full beard. Carved mermaids and monsters lurk on the choir-stall misericords (undersides).

The last major architectural additions were the prominent west twin towers, designed in 1698 by Sir Christopher Wren and com-

"IN LONDON LIES A KNIGHT A POPE INTERRED."

—*The Da Vinci Code*

Fleet Street (left) built its reputation on journalism, sensational scandalmongering, and pubs (above).

The ancient warrens of streets that make up The Temple (left) are punctuated by gardens (above). To medieval knights, the Temple Church was not just a reminder of Jerusalem, it was Jerusalem (right).

In the Temple Church lie the rows of knights' effigies (below). From St. James's Park (right) you can see the towers of Langdon and Sophie's next target, Westminster Abbey.

GILBERT·MARSHAL
fourth Earl of Pembroke (died 1241)

*The research room at
King's College (above)
is hushed and handsome.
Not far from London is
the global Prime
Meridian or Rose Line (right).*

Stepping across the threshold into Westminster Abbey, Langdon felt the outside world evaporate with a sudden hush." —*The Da Vinci Code*

In Westminster Abbey (below), you can seek out Newton's tomb (top left), dozens of memorials to the great and good, the College Garden (top center), and the octagonal Chapter House (top right).

Rosslyn Chapel teems with carvings (left), including pagan symbols (top left) and mysterious motifs (top right). Some of the most striking elements are the ornate pillars (above) near the Lady Chapel.

pleted in 1745. Fortunately, the abbey escaped major damage during World War II, as 60,000 sandbags protected the royal tombs.

Bones & Stones: Who's Buried in the Abbey?

There's a special sort of A-list for Westminster Abbey, and it has nothing to do with fame or wealth: it's the A-list for burial sites. Permission for burial here must be granted by the Dean of Westminster. To be eligible, a burial hopeful must have served the abbey or been an eminent British person who was outstanding in his or her field. Around 3,300 people have been buried in the abbey. (It's difficult to determine an exact number, as proper burial registers were not kept until 1607.) You might think that the abbey rattles with old bones, but in fact most of the interments are ash-filled urns.

The burial stones of the great and the good are grouped generally by their fields of expertise. (A map pinpointing each location is included in the guides sold in the abbey's bookshop.) Some of the most celebrated include composers (George Frederic Handel, Henry Purcell), writers and poets (Geoffrey Chaucer, Edmund Spenser, Samuel Johnson, Charles Dickens, Robert Browning, Alfred Lord Tennyson, Rudyard Kipling), and actors (David Garrick, Laurence Olivier, Dame Peggy Ashcroft). In the South Transept you'll find architects (Robert Adam, Sir George Gilbert Scott), while in the center of the nave, North Transept, lie politicians (William Pitt and Pitt the Younger, William Gladstone, Neville Chamberlain, Clement Atlee). Military figures close ranks in the nave South Aisle (Prince Rupert of the Rhine, Admiral Sir Clowdisley Shovell). In the central nave are scientists and engineers (Sir Isaac Newton, Charles Darwin) plus the explorer David Livingstone and philosopher William Wilberforce, who fought against the slave trade.

Thomas Parr gets the honors for the longest life; his nickname, Old Parr, is quite the understatement as he was said to be 152 years and 9 months at his death in 1635. You can find his white marble gravestone in the center of the South Transept. (If you're curious about this centenarian, you can see him in several portraits at the National Portrait Gallery.)

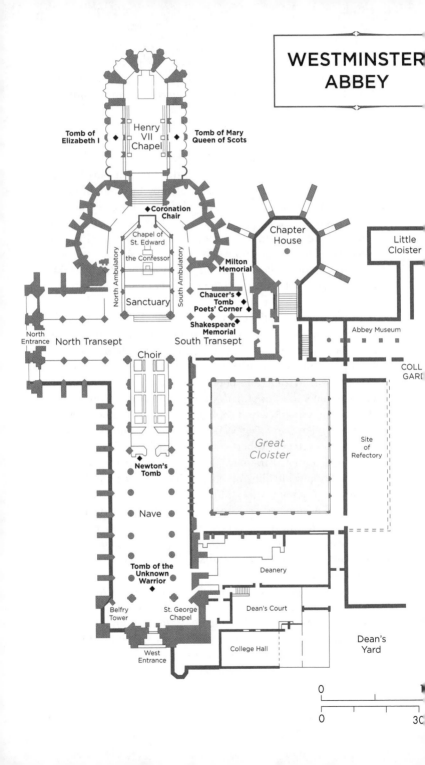

WESTMINSTER ABBEY

Tomb of Elizabeth I

Henry VII Chapel

Tomb of Mary Queen of Scots

◆ **Coronation Chair**

Chapel of St. Edward the Confessor

North Ambulatory

South Ambulatory

Milton Memorial

Sanctuary

Chaucer's Tomb
Poets' Corner ◆

Shakespeare Memorial ◆

Chapter House

Little Cloister

Abbey Museum

North Entrance

North Transept

South Transept

COLL GARD

Choir

Newton's Tomb

Great Cloister

Site of Refectory

Nave

Tomb of the Unknown Warrior ◆

Deanery

Belfry Tower

St. George Chapel

Dean's Court

Dean's Yard

West Entrance

College Hall

0

0   30

Poets' Corner

eoffrey Chaucer was the first poet to be buried in this corner of the abbey. Contrary to what you might expect, it wasn't his great work *Canterbury Tales* that got him the burial place in 1400, but his less glamorous day job as Clerk of Works to the Palace of Westminster. In the following centuries, Poets' Corner filled up with burials and memorials for authors and dramatists, followed by musicians and actors. (They eventually overflowed into the South Transept.) Among those memorialized are John Milton, Jane Austen, and William Wordsworth. The remains of Charles Dickens are here too. Those with somewhat scandalous reputa-

tions, such as Byron, took a little longer to find a place here after death. The best time to pore over these great names is early in the day, when you're less likely to be elbowed in this most popular area of the abbey.

Cheek-by-jowl memorials.

Memorable Monuments

The burials of artists and sovereigns usually provide the most interesting Westminster monuments and tales. Compare, for instance, the discreet burial of Elizabethan poet and dramatist Ben Jonson with the flamboyant one of actor David Garrick, who became famous playing most of Jonson's leading roles. Poor old Ben, once a pupil at Westminster's school, begged for 18 inches of ground in the abbey, which was all he could afford, and for that he had to be interred standing up in 1637. His stone reads "O rare Ben Jonson," a modest pun on the Latin *orare,* "to pray for." Garrick, meanwhile, got a dramatic statue near Poets' Corner.

William Shakespeare looks every inch the pensive producer with his elbow on his books. Almost a century after Shakespeare's death, Garrick pushed for this fine memorial, although the playwright's remains remained in his hometown, Stratford. At the funeral of another Elizabethan poet, Edmund Spenser, in 1559, his fellow scribes (probably including Shakespeare) threw their pens and elegies into his grave.

Size matters, especially if you're a sovereign, as demonstrated by the ornate marble tomb shared by Elizabeth I and Mary I in the North Aisle of Henry VII's Chapel (or Lady Chapel). The tomb was erected by Elizabeth's successor James I in 1606, three years after her death. The Protestant Queen Elizabeth kept the high ground even in death over Mary, her Catholic half-sister. "Bloody" Mary suffered the ignominy of being buried beneath her "heretic" half-sister. James then topped this with a more grandiose tomb for his mother (and Elizabeth I's rival), Mary Queen of Scots, in the parallel South Aisle. Hardly a surprise, since Elizabeth I had signed his mother's death warrant.

In Innocents' Corner you'll find the poignant memorials for James I's two young daughters; one tomb is modeled as a cradle. Here you'll also find the funerary urn for the infamous princes in the tower, Edward V and Richard, Duke of York. Mystery surrounds the death of these boys; they were supposedly murdered in the Tower of London on the orders of their uncle, Richard III, in 1483.

During the 17th century, the allocation of abbey space became a little lax. For instance, rogue gentleman Thomas Thynne got in even after being murdered by hired hit men in 1682 after a romantic scandal. His tomb, which was erected regardless of his dubious virtue, shows the scene of the crime.

Blood-red paper poppies fringe a simple slab of black marble at the western end of the nave: the Unknown Warrior's Tomb. Beneath lie soil from France and an unknown soldier, buried here on November 11, 1920. This powerful concept of remembrance was the first grave of its kind and is now echoed all over the world.

Treasures of the Abbey

The Confessor's shrine contains the holy bones and relics of St. Edward, probably the most precious and sacred objects in the abbey. Age and pilfering pilgrims have damaged its colored mosaic decoration of geometric triangles and circles. Because of the risk of further erosion, the shrine can only be admired from a distance as you walk around the medieval royal tombs that encircle it. You can see another, larger example of these rare mosaics in the

A Man of Gravity

*N*ewton's tomb looms large in the abbey's nave. Sculpted by J. M. Rysbrack in 1731 to a design by William Kent, it commemorates Newton's death in 1727. (On the tomb itself the year of death appears as 1726, which is correct according to the old Julian calendar that marked March 25th as the start of the year.)

The philosopher and mathematician reclines in flowing Grecian robes. Kent left nothing to creative chance, using mathematical calculations to balance the diagonal folds of the garment in relation to Newton's poised legs. A pair of putti dance attendance, holding a scroll illustrating one of Newton's mathematical inventions. The yellow globe hovering above is crammed with a Wedgwood-like relief of zodiac signs and constellations, including the route of a comet plotted by Newton in 1680. Topping the globe is the pensive figure of the goddess of astronomy. The sarcophagus beneath shows cheeky cherubs messing with a telescope and prism and working at the Royal Mint, of which Newton was Master. Take a closer look at the top right corner of the arch surrounding the tomb and you'll spot a *Code*-worthy emblem: a five-petaled blossom.

1268 pavement of the Sanctuary, which is thought to depict heaven and earth. This ancient style of work is named after the Italian Cosmati family who made it their specialty.

The Coronation Chair, at the foot of the Lady Chapel, has been the royal hot seat since King Edward I ordered it in 1300. It was made to contain the holy Stone of Scone, and did so for several hundred years until it was stolen by fervent Scots nationalists in 1950. Although it was returned a year later to the abbey, it was decreed that the stone should be kept at its rightful home at Edinburgh castle until needed for coronations.

Slightly less ancient—fast-forward to around 1398—is the earliest portrait of an English king. The artwork, showing Richard II at his coronation, hangs in the nave outside St. George's Chapel. The painting's colors are still striking, even after more than 600 years.

Head down to the undercroft to see the Abbey Museum's collection (as well as part of Edward's original Norman church).

Among the wax effigies, mementoes, and altarpieces, look out for the precious ring that Elizabeth I gave to her favorite, Essex. Their on-off romance has kept tongues wagging down through the centuries: did she or didn't she?

The Chapter House

Compared with the dim abbey, the octagonal Chapter House is a bright and sparkling place on sunny days. When light streams through its gigantic stained-glass windows, it plays upon the soaring central pillar from which the fan vaulting radiates and illuminates the precious wall paintings of gold and tin leaf, the best of their kind in England. Completed in 1259 as part of the abbey's Gothic rebuild, the Chapter House was used by the Benedictine monks. They would sit on the stone benches lining the room to hear the abbot's daily address of prayers and a chapter from the *Rules of Benedict*. Penances—sometimes flagellation—were administered against the central pillar, while younger novices were dealt with in the cloisters.

You won't find a heavy wooden door to the Chapter House as Langdon and Sophie did, but instead will pass through an ornate carved stone arch with a wrought-iron gate. Looking down, the glazed floor tiles give a taste of the more spectacular pavement in the Chapter House itself, where you'll find heraldic symbols galore. Check out the fleurs-de-lys, roses intertwined with a six-pointed star, leaves in the shape of the club suit from tarot cards (the scepters from the Royal Line, or Flowering Staff), and all variety of exotic beasts.

Painted roses and carved roses pop up everywhere in the abbey, but on the wall of the Chapter House is the most significant example. The inscription reads: "As the rose is the flower of flowers, so this is the house of houses." On the rose point, you should also know that the Tudor monarchs used a rose of red and white as a royal emblem. This two-colored rose represented the red House of Lancaster and the white House of York, who had fought for the crown of England for over 30 years. The victor of this War of the Roses was the Lancastrian Henry Tudor (Henry VII), who in 1485 united the warring houses by marrying Elizabeth of York. The "house of houses" phrase refers to the fact that the Chapter House was both a house of God and a house for the abbey's business. It was also used by early parliaments in the late 14th century, a precursor to the House of Commons.

Steeped as it is in symbolism, the Chapter House seems a perfect place for the dramatic showdown between Teabing, Langdon, and Sophie. Unlike Langdon, though, you won't be able to see the College Garden through the windows. The stained glass obscures the view—and also, the garden is in another direction and down a couple of cloister passages.

College Garden

Tended by monks for more than 900 years, the garden was originally planted with medicinal plants and vegetables, of which fennel and hyssop are still grown. There was also a small orchard. Though you won't get an inspirational look at an apple tree (that was a bit of artistic license on Brown's part, as there aren't any fruit trees here anymore), you can see five tall plane trees planted over 150 years ago. To help salve the disappointment over the apples, you can enjoy the fragrant beauty of banks of roses in this tranquil open-air sanctuary.

Visiting the Abbey

✉ *Broad Sanctuary, Westminster, SW1, 020/7222–5152, www. westminster-abbey.org.* Ⓤ *Westminster.*

Visitors usually have to circulate through the abbey along a set route. For the record, you cannot do grave rubbings in the abbey. Also note that photography is not permitted anywhere in the abbey. If you have questions during a visit, stop by the information desk (the staff is well used to *Code* queries by now). The abbey sometimes closes for special services and other events, so call ahead to confirm its opening hours.

LONDON & ROSLIN

The Riddle of Rosslyn Chapel

LANGDON AND SOPHIE ARRIVE AT Rosslyn Chapel. This 15th-century wonder teems with intricate stone carvings. Plants, animals real and imaginary, people, cryptic symbols—these carvings cover the walls and pillars and flow across the ceiling. There are some explicitly pagan references among the lot, too. The chapel has long sparked speculation involving religious and Templar history, especially since it sits above a mysterious underground cavern.

INSIDE ROSSLYN CHAPEL

Rosslyn Chapel was famous long before *The Da Vinci Code*. There have always been Grail legends and stories attached to the place, and it has, over the years, attracted the attention of many people with alternative—in some cases, downright wacky—views on religion and history. The interior of the church positively froths with exquisite stone carvings that marry Christian thought with pagan symbolism; many of the carvings are also said to relate to Freemasonry and the Knights Templar. It was this age-old reputation that made Langdon pause and reflect that Rosslyn was "far too obvious a location" for the Grail to be hidden in.

The derivation of the name Rosslyn has everything to do with the chapel's location, but not with the Rose Line as the *Code* claims. The chapel sits on a *ross*, or promontory, above a *lyn*, meaning a stream. The building is almost on the same north/south meridian as Glastonbury, which lies at least 14 miles further east.

One connection Brown didn't include—perhaps it is too tenuous to bear any great scrutiny—is the chapel's dedication to St. Matthew. In the *Code*, Brown relates how, in the Gospel of Philip (one of the Nag Hammadi texts) Peter disapproves of Mary Magdalene. Matthew was the only disciple who seemed to acknowledge her significance, saying that if the Savior made her worthy, then she shouldn't be rejected.

The chapel sits in Chapel Loan, to the east of the pleasant if unprepossessing village of Roslin in Midlothian (Rosslyn is the name of the chapel, Roslin is the name of the village). If walking toward the church, take a look at the orange-washed building in the lane before entering the churchyard. This was at one time the Old Rosslyn Inn, with a date over the door of 1660. It used to host visitors to the chapel, among them Samuel Johnson, James Boswell, Robert Burns, Sir Walter Scott, and William and Dorothy Wordsworth. It's not a stretch to think that the inn might have been the inspiration for the fieldstone house where Sophie's grandmother lived.

The main entrance to the chapel is the north door, though it's hard to tell given that the entire chapel is covered in scaffolding (and will be until late 2006 and perhaps beyond). In *The Da Vinci Code* both Langdon and Sophie pass the west wall to get to it, though this is stretching the truth somewhat, as the path from the Stables (the building containing the pay station, shop, and tearoom) leads straight to the door. At one time the north door was known as the Bachelor Door, as this was the entrance for men. The south door, now little used, was the entrance for women.

As you enter the churchyard, the first thing that strikes you about Rosslyn Chapel is its size. The choir is no more than 48 feet long, 18 feet wide (not including the side aisles) and 44 feet high (though some sources say just over 40 feet). To the east is the Lady Chapel with its six altars, which adds another seven-and-a-half feet to its length. On either side are the aisles, and at the southeast corner are steps down into the sacristy, which lies well below the level of the main church. The baptistery, which juts out beyond the west wall, is a Victorian addition, with an organ loft above it.

The novel notes that the chapel was built as an exact copy of Solomon's Temple in Jerusalem, and that the west wall is one aspect of this copy. In fact, Rosslyn was founded in 1446 by William St. Clair, third and last Prince of Orkney, as a college for secular priests, but the boundary wall wasn't built until 1736. St. Clair intended Rosslyn to consist of a chancel, a central tower, and a great nave to the west, but he died in 1484 before it could be finished. His son Oliver, having dutifully finished off the chancel, closed off its west end by building a rather plain wall. In the 19th century the foundations of the nave were uncovered, showing that, had the building been finished, it would have been the size of St. Giles Cathedral in Edinburgh.

There is, as noted in the *Code*, a massive vault below the chapel. In fact, radar scans have indicated the presence of several sizeable underground vaults, but the chambers' contents remain a mystery. No invasive work has been done, and the Rosslyn Chapel Trust, which oversees the site, has no plans to excavate. In the past few years various groups, including a Knights Templar organization, have stepped up requests to investigate further with ultrasound equipment, but to no avail. There are all kinds of theories about what the vaults could hold, ranging from the possible (tombs for the St. Clair family) to the out-there (Templar treasure or ancient Christian texts). On the other hand, Simon Beattie, director of the Rosslyn Chapel Trust, has said "I just don't think that there's really very much here to find."

Pillars of the Earth

Even without the *Code* connections, the interior of the building is spectacular. As Dan Brown wrote, "it's symbology heaven," which is what makes a visit so rewarding. It looks as though no stone here has escaped a mason's chisel.

Two of the most eye-catching elements are the Mason's Pillar and Apprentice Pillar, which stand between the chancel and the Lady Chapel. Langdon explains to Sophie that the two pillars are reproduced in modern Masonic temples and are known as Boaz and Jachin, respectively. A plainer third pillar, known as the Journeyman's Pillar, stands between the Mason's and the Apprentice. The Apprentice Pillar is the easternmost pillar in the south arcade. It's the most ornate of the three—exuberantly carved with spirals of foliage rising up round the column. The Mason's Pillar is to the north, and while its carving is intricate, it is more restrained.

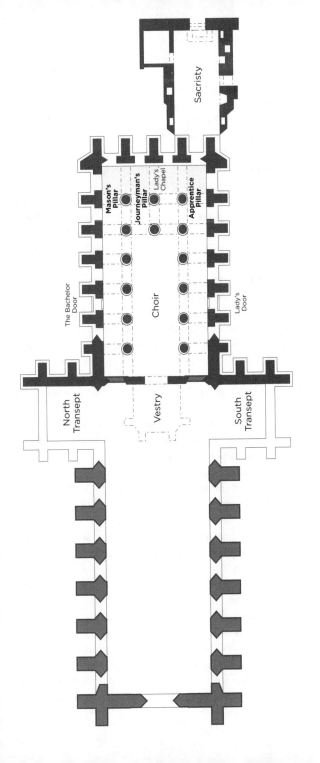

Sacristy

Mason's Pillar

Journeyman's Pillar

Lady's Chapel

Apprentice Pillar

The Bachelor Door

Choir

Lady's Door

Vestry

North Transept

South Transept

ROSSLYN CHAPEL

A legend attached to the pillars has echoes in Freemasonry. William St. Clair wanted the south arcade's pillar carved in a certain manner, and the master mason declared that he could not do it until he had studied similar pillars in Rome. So the master mason set off abroad, but when he returned he found that his apprentice had carved the column in his absence. Consumed with jealousy at the wonderful craftsmanship, he killed the apprentice by striking him on the head with his mallet.

On the west wall are carved two heads: to the south that of the apprentice, with the wound on his head clearly visible, and to the north that of the master mason. The legend recalls that of Hiram Abif, the master mason of Solomon's Temple who was supposedly killed for refusing to divulge the secrets of his craft. Abif's story features in one of the rituals of Freemasonry, when a candidate is elevated to the degree of master mason.

The Apprentice Pillar has one final secret to divulge. Around its base are carved the eight dragons of Neifelheim, which curled round the base of the Nordic tree of life that enclosed heaven, earth, and hell. The pillar may, in fact, be a representation of this tree, and William's connections with Orkney, which was controlled by Norway for more than 600 years, may account for this pagan symbolism.

There are plenty of other fascinating carvings in the chapel that weren't mentioned in the *Code*. The Green Man, a pagan symbol representing fertility, sprouts up in several places. The best example is in the Lady Chapel where one of the bosses, between the second and third altars, has the grimacing face of a man surrounded by foliage.

Perhaps the most intriguing carvings from a historical point of view are those over one of the windows in the south aisle wall. These carvings clearly show corn from North America, carved at least 46 years before Columbus landed in the New World. How were the masons able to depict it? Legend provides an explanation.

Sir Henry Sinclair, the first Prince of Orkney and grandfather of William, was supposed to have set out from Orkney in 1398 on a great voyage westwards with 200 men. They landed first in Newfoundland and then Nova Scotia, where they wintered with the Mi'kmaq Indians. The following year they set sail for home, but were driven south by strong winds, landing in present day Massachusetts, before making it back across the Atlantic. If the legend is true, it explains how Sir William knew about Indian corn and had carvings of it incorporated into the chapel.

One of the chapel's enigmatic codes seems to have recently been cracked. In October 2005, Scottish composer Stuart Mitchell announced that after 20 years of work he had deciphered the meaning of the carved cubes on the chapel's ceiling. He deduced that the symbols represented cadences and that they indicated music for a variety of instruments, from bagpipes to a trumpet. He has compared the sound to a nursery rhyme.

You can forget any feelings of hushed, solemn spirituality within Rosslyn Chapel. The space is invariably crowded with people, most milling around with guidebooks in hand. Sophie and Langdon enter the building just as the last guided tour of the day is finishing, and indeed guided tours are offered. However, there is no Star of David pathway on the floor made by countless feet as they move between the six key architectural points of the building. Rosslyn is still a working church and its seating means that walking in straight lines in a star pattern would be impossible.

Crowds of gawkers may not be your cup of tea, but in a sense the *Code* has done Rosslyn Chapel a favor. The novel has drawn attention to one of the great wonders of medieval architecture. Whether you visit it as a mystery fan, as an architecture buff, or as a skeptic, it's impossible to deny its allure when confronted with its carvings and cryptic symbolism.

Visiting Rosslyn Chapel

0131/440–2159, www.rosslyn-chapel.com.

Rosslyn Chapel sits six miles south of Edinburgh city center on the B7006, just off the A701 route to Peebles. For transportation details, *see* the On the Road with *The Da Vinci Code* chapter.

The Rosslyn Chapel Trust publishes an excellent guidebook (*Rosslyn Chapel*, £3.95) that takes you around the features in a logical manner and has photographs to help you identify some of the hard-to-find ones. It's helpful to bring a small pair of binoculars on a visit, as well as a small, unobtrusive flashlight. The church is very dim, so it can be easy to miss some of its details in the gloom. Please note that the exterior of the chapel is undergoing renovation and will be covered with scaffolding until late 2006 at the earliest.

on the road with
the da vinci code

SO YOU'RE OFF TO PARIS, ENGLAND, OR ITALY— or maybe all three! As well as seeing some of *The Da Vinci Code*-related sights on your trip, you could make your experience even more fun with the following recommendations. Here are our suggestions for places to eat, stay, and visit in each of the novel's key destinations. Each selection has a *Code* connection, be it one of location, history, atmosphere, or quirky coincidence. Working these choices into your itinerary is a surefire way to enhance your trip—even if you're an armchair traveler. Bon voyage!

PARIS

Phone numbers are listed below with their local area codes. When dialing from abroad, drop the initial "0" from the local area code. The country code for France is 33. Paris is six hours ahead of Eastern Standard Time.

Paris is divided into 20 arrondissements (districts). These arrondissements are laid out in a spiral, beginning from the area around the Louvre (the 1er arrondissement), then moving clockwise outward. When getting an address or checking directions or a map, it's key to have the arrondissement number of your destination.

A *Da Vinci Code* Itinerary

Following is a suggested itinerary for seeing all the main sights associated with *The Da Vinci Code*. The route is devoted to the novel; if you have more time, add a few extra days in the major capitals to explore them more fully. You'll find contact info for the sights in the Paris, Rome & the Vatican, London & Roslin, and On the Road With *The Da Vinci Code* chapters.

Day 1: Fly to Paris.

Day 2: Since you may be fighting jet lag, stick to shorter activities that will give you a chance to stretch your legs and get some fresh air. Walk between some of the novel's key sights; on the Right Bank, you can stroll from the place Vendôme to the Palais Royal to the Tuileries Gardens. Cross to the Left Bank to visit St-Sulpice. Later in the day, you could return to the place Vendôme for tea or a drink at the Ritz Paris, or window-shop your way up the Champs-Elysées.

Day 3: Time for the Louvre, where you could spend hours in the Denon Wing alone. Pace yourself! And remember that the Louvre is closed Tuesday but does have late-night hours on Monday and Wednesday.

Day 4: Drive out to Château Villette. You could even rent a Sophie-esque SmartCar for the trip; two companies that have them are EasyCar (www.easycar.com) and the Swiss company Elite Rent-a-Car (41–22–909–8787, www.eliterent.com).

Extra day? Head to the Loire Valley to visit Amboise and Clos Lucé, Leonardo's final home. At Clos Lucé, check out the working models of Leonardo's inventions. You can get to Amboise by car, via the A10, or by train, which takes about two hours. For train information, check the SNCF Web site (www.ter-sncf.com and find the Pays de la Loire). You can reach Amboise's tourism office at 02–47–57–01–37 or www.amboise-valdeloire.com.

Day 5: Hop an early flight to Rome (roughly two hours). Zip over to Vatican City to be gobsmacked by St. Peter's Basilica, the Sistine Chapel, and the astounding art in the Vatican Museums (including Leonardo's *St. Jerome*).

ON THE ROAD WITH *THE DA VINCI CODE*

Day 6: Take a day trip out to Castel Gandolfo. While the Papal Palace here is off-limits, it's still a lovely town to explore.

Day 7: Fly to Milan (just over an hour), home of Leonardo's *The Last Supper*. You can also take a train, but this will take five to six hours (www.trenitalia.com). You must make reservations with Santa Maria della Grazie in advance to see the painting. Call at least several days, if not a few weeks, ahead (02–89–42–11–46). Keep in mind that you'll only have a strictly enforced 15 minutes to inspect the *Supper*. Also, the site is closed Monday. But you can gaze at Leonardo's *Portrait of a Musician* for as long as you like at the Biblioteca Ambrosiana (02–80–69–21, www.ambrosiana.it).

Day 8: Fly to London. Light out for Fleet Street, The Temple, and Temple Church. After seeing the spooky tombs, brace yourself with a pint at a Fleet Street pub.

Day 9: Make your way to Westminster Abbey for a few hours among the tombs. From here it's a short walk to St. James's Park (pack some peanuts). Save some time for the National Gallery, where you can compare the *Virgin of the Rocks* painting here to the version you saw at the Louvre.

Day 10: On to Edinburgh, either by plane (about an hour and a half) or by train (nearly five hours, www.nationalrail.co.uk).

Day 11: Make the short trip out to Roslin, either by bus or by car. Rosslyn Chapel's intricate, teeming carvings will likely mesmerize

you for a couple of hours. Remember that the chapel's exterior is swathed in scaffolding until at least late 2006.

Day 12: Return home.

The Tuileries Gardens, Paris.

Where to Eat

Quoted prices are per person for a main course at dinner, or the equivalent.

Auberge Nicolas Flamel. Not only is this the oldest building in Paris (dating back to 1407), it was also the home to Nicolas Flamel, one of the world's most famous alchemists. Flamel supposedly discovered the secret of turning lead into gold; in the novel, he was named as a former Grand Master of the Priory of Sion. Today the restaurant maintains its medieval feel with its carved stone walls and exposed wooden beams. Typical French fare includes *magret de canard* and foie gras, accompanied by an impressive—if somewhat expensive—wine list. ⊠ *51 rue de Montmorency, the Marais, 3ᵉ arrondissement, 01–42–71–77–78.* Ⓜ *Arts-et-Métiers or Rambuteau.* €12–€19.

Bouillon Racine. After feeding your curiosity about the mysterious obelisk at St-Sulpice, feed your growling stomach at an authentic Art Nouveau worker's canteen just a few blocks away. Opened in 1904, this restaurant still retains its gorgeous mosaic tiling, paintings, mirrors, and floral motifs. The food is old-school hearty French fare like homemade onion soup and *pot au feu* (stew), and the service is extremely attentive. The crowd is more formal in the evening than at lunch; live jazz swings in on the weekends. ⊠ *3 rue Racine, St-Germain-des-Prés, 6ᵉ arrondissement, 01–44–32–15–60.* Ⓜ *Cluny-La Sorbonne or Odéon.* €15.

Café Denon. There are several places to catch a bite within the Louvre, including the large food court in the Carrousel du Louvre shopping center, but this tiny café is the best bet for escaping the crowds. The entrance is tricky to find, tucked behind the Roman Egypt room in the Denon Wing (only museum ticket holders have access). Its five outdoor tables overlook the Cour Denon, one of the museum's hidden courtyards, with a horseshoe-shaped staircase and tinkling fountain. ⊠ *Louvre Museum, Louvre/Tuileries, 1ᵉʳ arrondissement, 01–40–20–93–51.* Ⓜ *Palais-Royal.* €8.

Café Marly. Count the panes of glass in I. M. Pei's glass pyramid while sitting in this chic café overlooking the Louvre's courtyard. Because it's run by the Costes Brothers, known for their ultra-hip hotels and restaurants, this spot draws in the Parisian fashion

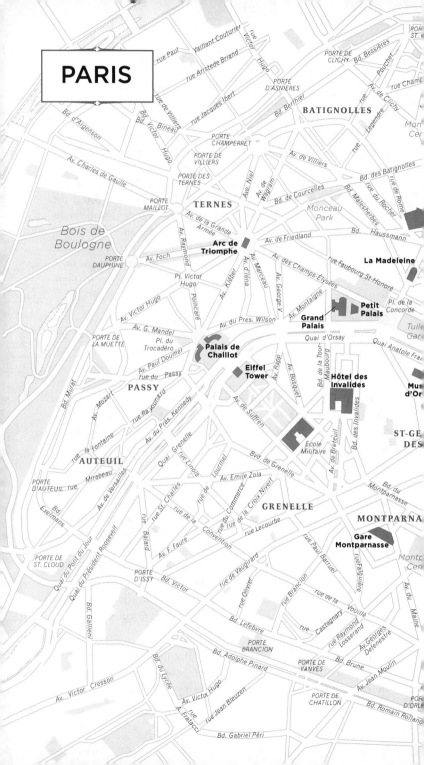

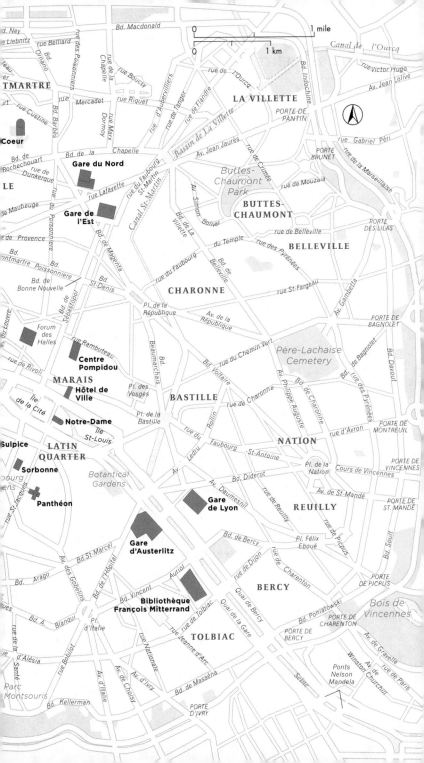

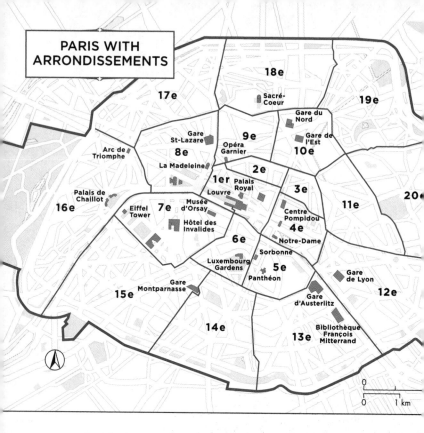

crowd, who meet here for morning coffee or evening apéritifs. Follow their lead and avoid going during mealtimes, or risk overpaying for the mediocre food. If all of the seats on the much-coveted terrace are taken, then console yourself with a table in the neo-Empire–style dining room, with glass windows overlooking the artworks of the Louvre's Richelieu Wing. ⊠ *Cour Napoléon du Louvre (enter from the Louvre courtyard), 93 rue de Rivoli, Louvre/Tuileries, 1er arrondissement, 01–49–26–06–60.* Ⓜ *Palais Royal. €8–€18.*

Café Terminus. This beautiful Belle Epoque brasserie across the street from the Gare St-Lazare is an ideal place for a meal or a drink while waiting for the train—or just to escape the bustling streets outside. Under the wing of a hotel, the classic 19th-century interior was given a smart touch-up by French fashion designer Sonia Rykiel. The creative and modern French dishes include sea bass and Normandy beef rib. If you order a *digestif*, ask to have it served in the hotel's lobby lounge, where you can relax in the armchairs and admire the historic marble arcades. ⊠ *Hôtel Concorde Saint-Lazare, 108 rue Saint-Lazare, Opéra/Grands Boulevards, 8ᵉ arrondissement, 01–40–08–43–30.* Ⓜ *St-Lazare. €23.*

L'Ecurie. The heavy wooden beams and ancient stone walls give this 17th-century stable house just behind the Panthéon plenty of Gallic character, while the friendly service and generous servings of sangria and Calvados make for a fun atmosphere. One of the best bets on the menu, which hasn't changed in almost a decade, is the saddle of lamb and salad with walnuts and blue cheese. The vaulted stone cellar with huge wooden tables is perfect for brainstorming groups looking for a bit of elbow room. ⊠ *2 rue Laplace, Latin Quarter, 5ᵉ arrondissement, 01–46–33–68–49.* Ⓜ *Cardinal Lemoine. €12–€18.*

Le Fumoir. This is one of the few Parisian establishments that successfully weathered its red-hot status when opening to become a steady favorite for its stylish bar and delicious food. Just behind the Louvre, it's the type of place where you might expect to see Sophie Neveu unwinding with a glass of wine at the bar or sequestering herself in the comfy reading room with a book and a café crème. On the menu you might find sea bass fillet with shiitake mushrooms or slices of zucchini layered with ricotta, spinach, and potato. The Sunday afternoon brunches (€21) are always packed with fashionably rumpled locals in sunglasses. ⊠ *6 rue de l'Amiral Coligny, Louvre/Tuileries, 1ᵉʳ arrondissement, 01–42–92–00–24.* Ⓜ *Louvre-Rivoli. €17–€26.*

Restaurant Le Meurice. This palace hotel restaurant faces the Tuileries Gardens where, barring any urgent investigative matters at the Louvre, the tree-lined paths are normally free of speeding Citroën police cars. The innovative French haute cuisine includes dishes such as crunchy veal sweetbreads with risotto and tarragon sauce and roasted duck foie gras with cherries and maple syrup. The magnificent dining room pulls out all the stops with mosaic tiling, marble walls, and crystal chandeliers. Leave room for the divinely light desserts. The three-course lunch menu with coffee is a relative steal at €75. ⊠ *228 rue de Rivoli, Louvre/Tuileries, 1ᵉʳ arrondissement, 01–44–58–10–10.* Ⓜ *Tuileries. €70–€110.*

ON THE ROAD WITH *THE DA VINCI CODE*

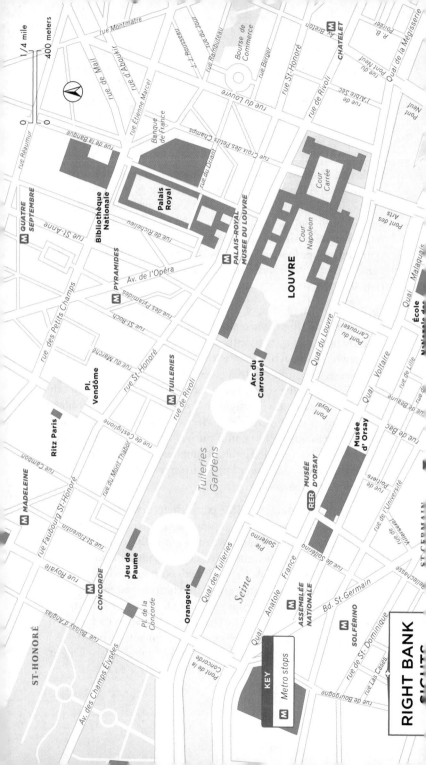

RIGHT BANK
SIGHTS

Restaurant du Palais Royal. Catch a glimpse of the bronze "Arago" medallion embedded in the pavement under the archway leading to the Palais Royal gardens when coming from the place Colette. Here you can enjoy the same garden view as the restaurant's illustrious neighbor, Le Grand Véfour, and have a far more affordable meal. Be sure to reserve a coveted place on the terrace when the weather's agreeable. ✉ *110 galerie de Valois, Louvre/ Tuileries, 1ᵉʳ arrondissement, 01–40–20–00–27.* Ⓜ *Palais-Royal.* €*18–*€*34.*

Taverne Henri IV. Captain Bezu Fache's agents would surely frequent this typical Parisian wine bar, just around the corner from the DCPJ headquarters on the Ile de la Cité. Run for over 50 years by the same family, this cheap and cheerful establishment serves a large selection of wines (purchased direct from the growers) by the glass, bottle, or pitcher, accompanied by *assiettes* of cheeses, cold meats, and paté. There are also tasty hot tarts and quiches to satisfy bigger appetites. ✉ *13 place du Pont Neuf, Ile de la Cité, 1ᵉʳ arrondissement, 01–43–54–27–90.* Ⓜ *Pont-Neuf or Cité.* €*12.*

Quick Bites

Marché Buci. One of the liveliest market streets in Paris, the Marché Buci is a few blocks from St-Sulpice church. Pick up the fixings for a picnic from the open fruit stalls, butcher shops, and bakeries, or stop into one of the cafés or sandwich shops for a quick meal. ✉ *Corner of rue de Buci and rue de Seine, St-Germain-des-Prés, 6ᵉ arrondissement.* Ⓜ *Odéon or Mabillon.*

Pâtisserie Cador. This tearoom and pastry shop with the Versailles-like interior is an elegant retreat behind the Louvre. Stay for afternoon tea in the dainty dining room, or get a takeaway treat to eat while perusing the *bouquiniste* (second-hand bookseller) stalls along the Seine. ✉ *2 rue de l'Amiral-Coligny, Louvre/ Tuileries, 1ᵉʳ arrondissement, 01–45–08–19–18.* Ⓜ *Louvre-Rivoli.*

Pierre Hermé. There's often a line to get into this swanky pastry boutique around the corner from St-Sulpice. But patience always pays off when it comes to the amazing pastries with unusual flavors such as rose, white truffle, olive oil, and saffron. The chocolates, *macarons* (cream-filled meringue-like cookies), and his signature *2000 Feuilles* are all beautifully packaged for that much-

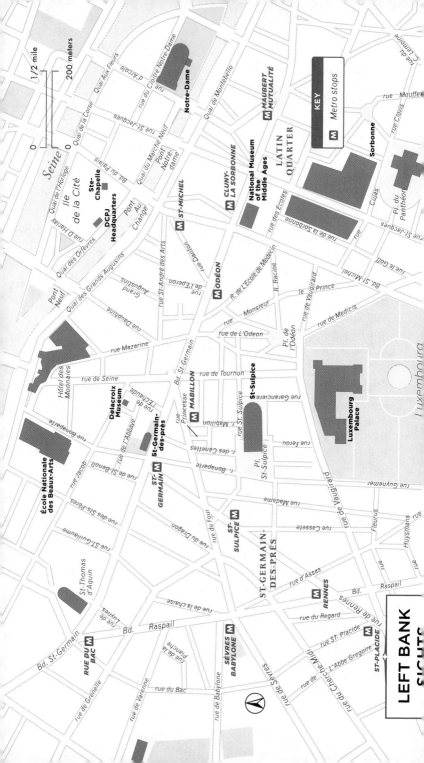

needed injection of sugar on the go. ✉ *72 rue Bonaparte, St-Germain-des-Prés, 6ᵉ arrondissement, 01–43–54–47–77.* Ⓜ *St-Sulpice.*

Where to Stay

Quoted prices are for a standard double room in high season, including tax (19.6%).

Esprit St-Germain. If making a reservation here, be sure to request a room with views over St-Sulpice church, the scene of Silas's murderous search for the hidden keystone. Opened in late 2004, this sleek, trendy boutique hotel is a study in luxurious textures. Leather, velvet, and slate are combined in a neutral color palette and punctuated by dramatic contemporary artworks. Guest rooms are equipped with flat-screen TVs, cordless phones, and high-speed Internet access. Head to the top floor for the steam room, sauna, and fitness machines, or curl up with a complimentary drink in the hotel's fireplace lounge. ✉ *22 rue St-Sulpice, St-Germain-des-Prés, 6ᵉ arrondissement, 01–53–10–55–55, www. espritsaintgermain.com.* Ⓜ *St-Sulpice or Mabillon.* €290–€350.

Hôtel Henri IV. Just off the western tip of the Ile de la Cité, where the Knights Templar were burned at the stake in 1314, is this rock-bottom budget hotel hidden in the tree-lined place Dauphine. Once home to King Henri IV's printing presses, the 17th-century building isn't for the faint of heart. It's got a creaky, narrow staircase (five flights, no elevator) and scruffy rooms *sans* TV, telephone, or a/c. You'll pay a slightly higher rate for a room with toilet and shower or tub; otherwise, be prepared to schlep your towel and shampoo down the hallway to the shared facilities. Despite these hurdles, the excellent location and a steady influx of hardy travelers keep this hotel packed year-round, so book early! ✉ *25 place Dauphine, Ile de la Cité, 1ᵉʳ arrondissement, 01–43–54–44–53.* Ⓜ *Cité or Pont-Neuf.* €33–€71.

Hôtel Relais Saint-Sulpice. Wake up to the sound of the solemn bells of St-Sulpice church, which is right behind this stylish hotel. A reception area done in an eclectic mix of ethnic artworks and deco furnishings leads to the elegant, understated rooms set around an ivy-clad courtyard. Breakfast is served in a bright dining room beneath the glass garden atrium, and the wood-paneled sauna is the perfect place to relax. ✉ *3 rue Garancière, St-Germain-des-Prés, 6ᵉ arrondissement, 01–46–33–99–00, www.relais-saint-sulpice.com.* Ⓜ *St-Sulpice.* €170–€190.

Hôtel St-Merry. On a bustling pedestrian street right in the center of Paris, this stunning Gothic boutique hotel was once the presbytery of the adjacent St-Merry church. Its 17th-century stone walls, thick wooden beams, stained glass, and church pew benches give each of the 11 rooms the feel of a medieval abbey. In room 9, you'd even get to sleep beneath one of the giant stone buttresses supporting the church. And Silas the monk would surely approve of the hotel's ascetic lack of 21st-century luxuries like televisions and an elevator. ✉ *78 rue de la Verrerie, Beaubourg/Les Halles, 4ᵉ arrondissement, 01–42–78–14–15, www.hotelmarais.com.* Ⓜ *Châtelet or Hôtel de Ville.* €160.

Hôtel Westminster Opéra. Visiting academics may feel more at home in this discreet luxury hotel near the place Vendôme than at the glitzy Ritz. As the name indicates, the hotel has been hosting the Duke of Westminster since it was his private Parisian pied-à-terre in the late 19th century. Period furnishings, marble fireplaces, and crystal chandeliers emphasize the regal atmosphere, and a glass-topped fitness center and steam room offer you views over the Paris rooftops. With Wi-Fi access, the top-notch Céladon restaurant, and live piano music in the British-style Duke's Bar, you might find it hard to leave this cozy cocoon. ✉ *13 rue de la Paix, Opéra/Grands Boulevards, 2ᵉ arrondissement, 01–42–61–57–46, www.hotelwestminster.com.* Ⓜ *Opéra.* €270–€420.

Relais du Louvre. One of the best deals in central Paris, this hotel's charming decor and convenient location right behind the Louvre have earned it a loyal following among savvy travelers. Rooms have exposed wooden beams and simple floral print decoration, with the largest ones facing the inner courtyard and the smaller ones facing the street with views of the museum and the dramatic St-Germain-l'Auxerrois church next door. Families can take advantage of the roomy top-floor apartment for four, equipped with a large kitchen. ✉ *19 rue des Prêtres St-Germain-l'Auxerrois, Louvre/Tuileries, 1ᵉʳ arrondissement, 01–40–41–96–42, www.relaisdulouvre.com.* Ⓜ *Louvre-Rivoli.* €150–€190.

Places to See & Shop

Au Nom de la Rose. Taking its name from Umberto Eco's murder mystery novel, this florist sells nothing but roses. You can muse on the rose's Grail symbolism while browsing the long-stemmed beauties in zinc buckets in this petal-strewn boutique. Rustic stone walls and exposed wooden beams make it especially atmospheric. The boxes of soap rose petals make great souvenirs. ⊠ *4 rue de Tournon, St-Germain-des-Prés, 6ᵉ arrondissement, 01–46–34–10–64.* Ⓜ *St-Sulpice.*

Basilica St-Denis. You'll have to go a bit off the beaten path to visit the royal necropolis of France, where all but three French monarchs since the Merovingian King Dagobert in the 7th century have been buried. When Teabing spells out his Grail theories to Sophie, she recalls the story of Dagobert, who was stabbed through the eye and killed. (According to Teabing, the Merovingian bloodline goes back to Christ, and Dagobert's assassination had been arranged by the Vatican.) The basilica was built in the 12th century, replacing an earlier 5th-century church containing the crypt of St-Denis, martyred patron saint of France. It's considered one of the finest examples of early Gothic architecture in Europe. ⊠ *1 rue de la Légion d'Honneur, St-Denis, 01–48–09–83–54.* Ⓜ *Basilique St-Denis.*

Delacroix Museum. Captivated by the two Eugène Delacroix frescoes in the St-Sulpice church? Get a more intimate view of the artist's works a few blocks away at his last residence on the charming place Furstenburg. Turned into a museum after the painter's death in 1863, it offers an intimate look at the artist's paintings as well as his personal souvenirs, letters, and photos. ⊠ *6 rue de Furstenburg, St-Germain-des-Prés, 6ᵉ arrondissement, 01–44–41–86–50.* Ⓜ *St-Germain-des-Prés.*

L'Art Liturgique. This is one of several boutiques on the square facing St-Sulpice specializing in religious artworks. Browse the icons, statues, religious jewelry, rosaries, handcrafted nativity scenes, and handmade *santons* (creche figures) from Provence. ⊠ *4 rue du Vieux Colombier, St-Germain-des-Prés, 6ᵉ arrondissement, 01–45–48–71–04.* Ⓜ *St-Sulpice.*

Mona Lisait. The name's a play on words that means "Mona Reads." Besides discount books you'll find scads of cheap post-

Code-Theme Walking Tours

*T*he following companies offer *Da Vinci Code* walking tours. Standard tours last 2 to 2½ hours.

■ **Paris Muse** (06–73–77–33–52, www.parismuse.com). Art historians take small groups (four people max) through the Louvre, focusing on Leonardo's paintings, depictions of Mary Magdalene, and symbolic representations of feminine divinity.

■ **Paris Walks** (01–48–09–21–40, www.paris-walks.com). Regularly scheduled (and inexpensive) walks visit the key sights described in the novel, including St-Sulpice, the Palais Royal, and the Louvre pyramids. Special tours of the Louvre are also occasionally scheduled or can be privately booked.

Tracking the Rose Line.

cards. ⊠ *9 rue St-Martin, Beaubourg-Les Halles, 1ᵉʳ arrondissement. 01–42–74–03–02.* Ⓜ *Châtelet.*

National Museum of the Middle Ages. Opened in 1843 in the 15th-century residence of the Cluny abbots, this museum highlights medieval arts and culture, including stained glass, altarpieces, stone and wood carvings, Gothic ivories, and the mesmerizing allegorical *Lady and the Unicorn* tapestries. Outside the museum walls are the ruins of Gallo-Roman baths dating back to the 2nd century A.D., and a medieval-themed garden open to the public. ⊠ *6 place Paul-Painlevé, Latin Quarter, 5ᵉ arrondissement, 01–53–73–78–00.* Ⓜ *Cluny-La Sorbonne.*

Variantes. Scoop up one of the carved wooden "secret boxes" sold at this tiny boutique—though you won't find a Saunière-esque cryptex inside. The shop is just a few blocks from St-Sulpice. Here you can also find chessboards, tarot and playing card decks in many themes (including *Mona Lisa*), and clever puzzles and games. ✉ *29 rue St-André-des-Arts, St-Germain-des-Prés, 6ᵉ arrondissement, 01–43–26–01–01.* Ⓜ *St-Michel.*

After Hours

Chez Georges. One of the oldest bars in the St-Sulpice area, this scruffy hole-in-the-wall is always packed with locals and students for the cheap wine and friendly atmosphere. Take your last breath of smoke-free air before descending into the cellar music bar, where bodies are jovially crammed around wooden tables and the tiny dance floor until the wee hours. ✉ *11 rue des Canettes, St-Germain-des-Prés, 6ᵉ arrondissement, 01–43–26–79–15.* Ⓜ *Odéon.*

Classical Music and Organ Concerts. Imagine hearing the sounds of Bach, Mozart, and Chopin in the majestic setting of Paris's historic cathedrals and churches like St-Sulpice, St-Germain-des-Prés, or Ste-Chapelle. Look for flyers posted on the church walls, or check listings at www.ampconcerts.com or www.parisinfo.com. You can also catch free organ recitals a half-hour before mass at Notre-Dame Cathedral and St-Eustache church.

Harry's New York Bar. Open since 1911, this historic wood-paneled bar between place Vendôme and the Opéra is covered in American university memorabilia and autographed photos from some of its more illustrious clientele. Langdon would feel right at home at the bar with the English-language newspapers during the quiet afternoons. The lower-level piano bar (where Gershwin composed *An American in Paris*) attracts a lively post-theater crowd well into the night. ✉ *5 rue Daunou, Opéra/Grands Boulevards, 2ᵉ arrondissement, 01–42–61–71–14.* Ⓜ *Opéra.*

Le Cab' Nightclub. Dance 'til dawn at the hippest club in town, Le Cab' (short for cabaret, not taxi cab). Overlooking the square between the Louvre and the Palais Royal, the club's futuristic interior pulls in a steady clientele of Parisian fashionistas and international jet-setters. Dress fabulously or book a table for dinner if you want to sail past the steely-eyed doormen. ✉*2 place du Palais Royal, Louvre/Tuileries, 1ᵉʳ arrondissement, 01–58–62–56–25.* Ⓜ *Palais-Royal.*

Live Jazz. Paris is one of the favorite cities of jazz lovers, attracting top acts from around the world. Classics include Le Bilboquet

---◇---

Best Bookstores for Learning More about Paris

■ **Galignani**. This elegant French-English bookshop opened in 1802 under the arches of the rue de Rivoli, facing the Louvre and the Tuileries gardens. They stock French literature, English travel guides, and international press. ✉ *224 rue de Rivoli, Louvre/ Tuileries, 1er arrondissement, 01–42–60–76–07.* Ⓜ *Tuileries.*

■ **Librairie de la Bibliothèque Historique de la ville de Paris**. The Bookstore of the History of Paris Library sells books about, no surprise, Paris! Here you'll find everything from detailed historic texts and architectural coffee-table books to little pocket guides and souvenir posters. ✉ *22 rue Malher, the Marais, 3e arrondissement. 01–44–59–29–68.* Ⓜ *St-Paul.*

■ **Village Voice**. A few blocks from St-Sulpice, this stellar bookstore sells contemporary anglophone books on two floors and holds regular readings of internationally renowned authors. The address seems ideal for Princesse Sophie. ✉ *6 rue Princesse, St-Germain-des-Prés, 6e arrondissement, 01–46–33–36–47.* Ⓜ *Odéon or St-Sulpice.*

(✉ 13 rue St-Benoît, St-Germain-des-Prés, 6e arrondissement, 01–45–48–81–84, Ⓜ St-Germain-des-Prés), near St-Sulpice church. Not far from the Louvre there's the Duc des Lombards (✉ 42 rue des Lombards, Beaubourg/Les Halles, 1er arrondissement, 01–42–33–22–88 Ⓜ Châtelet-Les Halles), a romantic Métro-inspired venue.

Opéra Garnier. Looking for more drama? Catch an opera, dance or theater production at the opulent Opéra Garnier, built in the late 19th century under Napoleon III. For those more interested in the marble-and-gilt interior, it's also possible to buy a visitor's ticket during the day to explore the monumental theater at your leisure. Sign up for one of the daily guided tours to hear about the original Phantom of the Opera. ✉ *Place de l'Opéra, 9e arrondissement. 01–40–01–22–63. (Tour information: 01–90–01–19–70.) www.opera-de-paris.fr.* Ⓜ *Opéra.*

OME & THE VATICAN

Phone numbers are listed below with their local area codes. The country code for Italy is 39. Italy is six hours ahead of Eastern Standard Time.

Where to Eat

Quoted prices are per person for a main course at dinner, or the equivalent.

L'Angolo Divino. This restaurant's endless selection of wines would satisfy the pickiest wine snob, even Sir Leigh Teabing. Accompanying the international ambrosias are delicious tapas-style dishes like *petto d'oca affumicato con ruchetta e pinoli* (goose paté with arugula and pine nuts). If you'd just like something to nibble with your vino, try some *formaggi* (cheese) and *salumi* (meat). ⊠ *Via dei Balestrari 12, Campo de' Fiori, 06–68–64–413.* €9.

Clemente alla Maddalena. All clues lead Langdon, Sophie, and Teabing to Mary Magdalene, so it's only fitting to pause for dinner at Clemente alla Maddalena. Here you can dine inside a sumptuous palazzo or on the patio facing Rome's only rococo church, Chiesa Santa Maria della Maddalena. The menu is seasonal; in spring and summer, for instance, you might find cherry octopus soup or *paccheri con astice e pomodorini* (pasta with lobster and tiny tomatoes) on the menu. ⊠ *Piazza della Maddalena 4, Pantheon, 06–68–33–633.* €14 *first course,* €22 *second course.*

Il Matriciano. It's easy to imagine Bishop Aringarosa here, perhaps with a gaggle of prelates in tow, enjoying some of the city's best traditional Roman cuisine, with dishes like spaghetti *alla carbonara* (with an egg and bacon sauce), *trippa* (tripe), and *coda alla vaccinara* (oxtail with celery). The assortment of *fritte* (fried antipasti)—zucchini flowers, olives, broccoli, *supplí* (rice balls with mozzarella in the center)—should not be missed. ⊠ *Via dei Gracchi, 55, San Pietro, 06–32–12–327.* €15 *first course,* €20 *second course.*

Taverna degli Amici. Relaxing among medieval and Renaissance architecture is one of Rome's great pleasures. Taverna degli Amici is one such place, a calm piazza with ivy-covered walls and a medieval tower. The menu offers typical dishes from the Lazio region that change depending on the mood of the chef. Expect favorites like *tonnarelli cacio e pepe* (tubular pasta with pecorino cheese and pepper). ⊠ *Piazza Margana 36/37, Ghetto, 06–69–92–06–37. €13 first course, €20 second course.*

Taverna Lucifero. The indulgent menu of pastas, fondues, and sweets here would disarm nearly any conspiracy theorist. Nestled in an archway off the noisy Campo de' Fiori, the tiny Taverna is this neighborhood's most romantic secret. All pastas are made daily—notably the *taglioni al tartufo bianco* (long pasta with white truffle)—and though the menu is ever-changing the selection of savory and sweet fondues remains the same. ⊠ *Via dei Cappellari 28, Campo de' Fiori, 06–68–80–55–36. €8 first course, €11 second course.*

Quick Bites

Caffè delle Arti. Attached to the Galleria Nazionale di Arte Moderna is a café that's lovely enough for even the most discerning curators. The grand terrace is edged by Corinthian columns, an ideal location for the requisite morning cappuccino. ⊠ *Via Gramsci 73, Villa Borghese, 06–88–4 –54–51.*

Ciampini. The selection of 12 to 14 homemade gelatos here is considered among the best in Rome. Sophie, code breaker and wannabe Formula 1 driver, would enjoy showing Langdon the SmartCar dealership at the far end of the piazza. ⊠ *Piazza San Lorenzo in Lucina 29, Pantheon, 06–68–76–606.*

Confetteria Moriondo e Gariglio. If Sister Sandrine had a sweet tooth and a little free time she'd surely drop by Moriondo e Gariglio, an old-style chocolate shop run by white-aproned women who look like nuns. ⊠ *Via de Pié di Marmo 21–22, Pantheon, 06–69–90–856.*

Where to Stay

Quoted prices are for a standard double room in high season, 9–12% tax included.

Albergo del Sole al Pantheon. Decorated in the splendid style of a 15th-century palazzo, Albergo del Sole is easily one of the most enchanting hotels in Rome. It's tucked away in Piazza Rotonda, overlooking the Pantheon, and is just a short stroll from the Trevi Fountain and the Spanish Steps. The 23 rooms are unique, but all have tapestries, colorful linens, and tiled floors. Try to book a suite facing the piazza—the views are amazing. ⊠ *Piazza della Rotonda 63, Pantheon, 06–67–80–441, www.hotelsolealpantheon. com. €260–€520.*

Argentina Residenza. This is the sort of place Bishop Aringarosa might stay when on Opus Dei business. The hotel is set in an 18th-century palazzo and has six spotless, comfortable, and stylish rooms. They're also soundproofed, as walls are made of thick concrete reinforced with wood paneling. The hotel is close to the city's major bus and tram lines, convenient for quick getaways. ⊠ *Via di Torre Argentina, 47, Largo Argentina, 06–68—19–32–67, www.argentinaresidenza.com. €120–€230.*

The Bee Hive. Owned by a couple from Southern California, The Bee Hive's seven rooms, dormitory, and three apartments are SoCal hip, with their light hues, modern furniture, and surf prints. The place stays busy, so it's best to book well in advance, especially if you're after one of the spacious apartments. ⊠ *Via Marghera, 8, Termini (Train Station), 06–44–70–45–53, www.the-beehive.com. €40–€70.*

Grand Hotel de la Minerve. Nab a room here and you can commune with a sacred feminine figure—the beautiful 17th-century palazzo sits atop the ruins of an ancient temple to Minerva. The service is impeccable, and the rooms so magnificent, you'll feel blessed to be here. The excellent Restaurant La Cesta serves dinner on the roof during summer, a treat since the views from the roof—especially of the dome of St. Peter's—are smashing. ⊠ *Piazza della Minerva 69, Pantheon, 06–69–52–01, www. grandhoteldelaminerve.com. €300–€425.*

Hotel Columbus. To sleep amidst Renaissance art, make your way to the Columbus in the Palazzo dei Penitenzieri, a mere 100 meters from St. Peter's Square. The understated 15th-century façade hides an exquisite hotel whose 92 individually decorated rooms have vaulted ceilings, wood panels, and frescoed walls by Pinturicchio and other late-15th-century painters. There's more Pinturicchio in the frescoed restaurant, which serves superb Ital-

ON THE ROAD WITH *THE DA VINCI CODE*

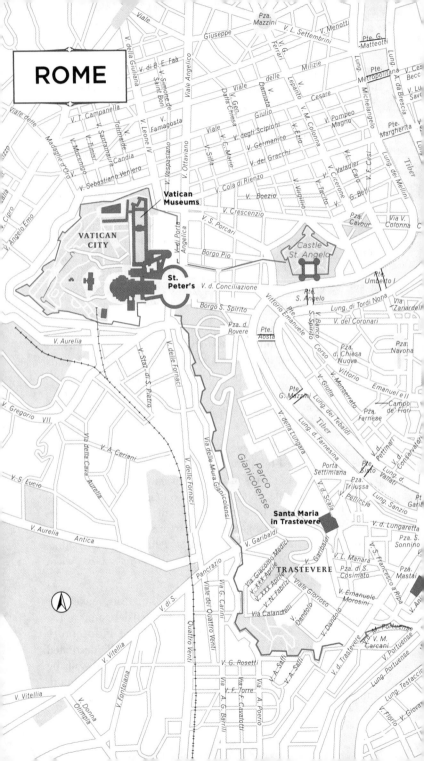

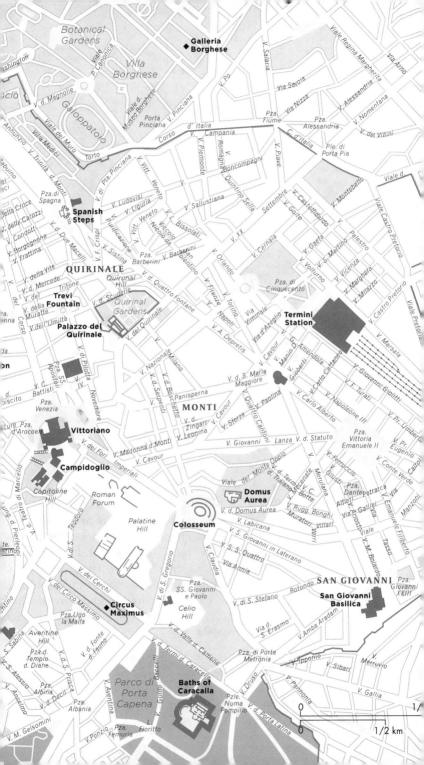

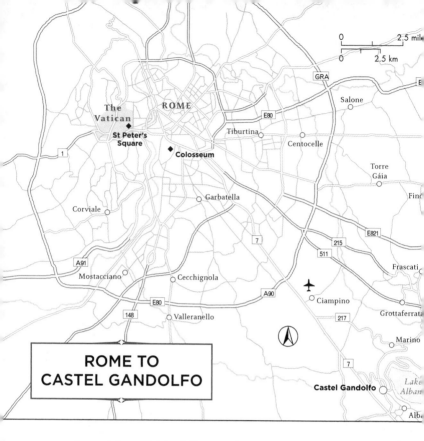

ROME TO CASTEL GANDOLFO

ian cuisine. ✉ *Via della Conciliazione 33, San Pietro, 06–68–65–435, www.hotelcolumbus.net.* €160–€320.

Hotel dei Consoli. If you'd like to be near the Vatican but not directly in the Pope's line of sight, stay at the lovely Hotel dei Consoli, a tasteful 26-room hotel in a 19th-century palazzo. Each floor has a different design scheme and name: Piano dei Mappamondi ("world maps"), Piano dei Fiori ("flowers"), and Piano delle Battaglie ("battles"). Bathrooms are lavishly decorated with marble and bronze fixtures, but are outdone by the exquisite wood-paneled bedrooms with colorful silk drapery and ultrafine linens. ✉ *Via Varrone 2/D, San Pietro, 06–68–89–29–72, www.hoteldeiconsoli.com.* €200–€400.

Hotel Teatro di Pompeo. For a bloodthirsty thrill, hit this intimate hotel, built on the remains of the Roman Teatro di Pompeo, where Caesar was murdered. The 33 rooms are simply furnished with wood-beam ceilings. The breakfast area, built into the exposed Roman ruins, is an intriguing setting. ⊠ *Largo del Pallaro 8, Campo de' Fiori, 06–68–72–812, www.hotelteatrodipompeo.it. €130–€190.*

Arts Attack

The Genius of Leonardo da Vinci. From January through October, the former tomb of Nero and presently the side wing of the Basilica Santa Maria del Popolo hosts an exhibit of inventions based on drawings from Leonardo notebooks. The flying machines are for display only, but there are lots of hands-on exhibits with cogwheels and gears to manipulate. ⊠ *Sala del Bramante, Piazza del Popolo, 06–36–00–42–24.*

***The Last Supper* Tapestry at Pinacoteca.** If you can't get to Milan to see Leonardo's *The Last Supper*, you can see a tapestry of it here, in the back room of the Pinacoteca at the Vatican Museums. Amidst three beautiful Raphael paintings and seven Raphael-designed tapestries is the *Last Supper* tapestry, woven by Flemish artists in the 16th century. ⊠ *Viale Vaticano, Vatican City, 06–69–88–49–47, http://mv.vatican.va.*

Roseto Comunale and Keyhole of Villa Malta. Each spring Rome opens the Roseto Comunale, a beautiful rose garden on the Aventine hill above the Circus Maximus. It's the perfect place to ponder rose symbolism and the sacred feminine—plus it also hosts readings, jazz performances, and other musical events. Walk up the hill (at via di Santa Sabina 3) and peek through the Knights of Malta keyhole for a charming view. The garden stays open from May through August. ⊠ *Via di Valle Murcia 6, Aventino, 06–57–46–810.*

Vatican Museums. The Sistine Chapel's ceiling, painted by Leonardo's rival Michelangelo, is the hot spot here. But there are many other Renaissance masterpieces to relish, like the Raphael Rooms. Raphael's work in the Stanza della Segnatura is especially illuminating, as it embodies the Renaissance interest in naturalism, humanism, and the classical world. And in the Pinacoteca (Picture Gallery) you can see Leonardo's unfinished painting *St. Jerome.* Remember that you must be wearing appropriate clothing to enter the Vatican Museums, which means no bare knees or shoulders. ⊠ *Main museum entrance, Viale Vaticano, 06–69–88–*

33–32 or 06–69–88–46–76 for guided visit reservations, www.vatican.va.

Where to Raise a Glass

Bar San Callisto. Although the bar isn't the most inviting space, the granita di caffè and hot chocolate here are delicious. It's a great late-night hang-out across the street from the Consiglio at Palazzo San Callisto (Vatican extra territory, with archives), so keep an eye out for Bishop Aringarosa. ⊠ *Piazza San Callisto 3, Trastevere, 06–58–35–869.*

Hotel Exedra. A fine place for an after-dinner drink is this gorgeous bar atop a 19th-century palazzo in Piazza Repubblica, near the ancient baths of Diocletian. With a glass of prosecco in hand, you'll find this the perfect place to unwind. ⊠ *Piazza Repubblica 47, Piazza Repubblica, 06–48–93–81.*

Orusdir Pub. Tales from the life of Orusdir, a medieval Scottish magician who fought against dark knights like Templarum, appear on the walls at this unusual pub. There's quite a magical-medieval vibe, with minstrels and troubadours performing nightly and tarot cards read weekly. ⊠ *Via dei Cappellari 130, Campo de' Fiori, 339–23–70–046.*

LONDON

Phone numbers are listed below with their local area codes. When dialing from abroad, drop the initial "0" from the local area code. The country code for Great Britain is 44. London is five hours ahead of Eastern Standard Time.

Where to Eat

Quoted prices are per person for a main course at dinner, or the equivalent.

The Admiralty. Set within stately Somerset House, The Admiralty is the perfect setting for a Teabing tea party. The pale blue decor, glittering chandeliers, and flawless silver place settings are the perfect expression of tempered decadence. The mostly French menu offers excellent seafood dishes and a succulent pot-roasted Barbary duck. If it's sunny out and you're in the mood for something light, try the outside bistro overlooking the Thames. ⊠ *Somerset House, the Strand, Covent Garden, WC2, 020/7845–4646.* U *Temple. £13–£28.*

Belgo Centraal. Although the waiters dress like monks at this busy Belgian restaurant, you're not likely to find an albino among the robed. Downstairs in the hectic dining room, tourists and trendy locals nosh on tasty Black Forest ham with pear chutney, mussels and Flemish fries, or chicken in creamy lemon sauce. The restaurant's lengthy list of microbrewery Belgian beers keeps things hopping most nights, especially on Friday and Saturday. Too many poisons to choose from? Try a taster, a rack of small glasses, each with a different brew. ⊠ *50 Earlham Street, Covent Garden, WC2, 020/7813–2233.* U *Covent Garden. £11–£19.*

Gay Hussar. You might recognize members of Tony Blair's cabinet here, or perhaps a glowering bishop plotting strategy over red wine and veal goulash. With its ivory walls and golden lighting, this popular Hungarian restaurant looks as if it were preserved in amber. The staff treats everybody like an MP, and with good reason: the walls are covered with photos of MPs who dine here. It's not far from Westminster Abbey, but far enough to make taking a taxi a good idea. ⊠ *2 Greek Street, Soho, W1, 020/7437–0973.* U *Tottenham Court Road. £18–£28.*

Oxo Tower Restaurant and Brasserie. You'll have no difficulties seeing the Middle Temple from the dining room here, on the eighth floor of the Oxo Tower on the South Bank. The kitchen turns out French-influenced British fare, like pan-fried guinea fowl with leeks, or roasted scallops with braised fennel in lemon olive oil. The bistro and bar are less expensive than the restaurant, and their sweeping views across the river are just as good. ⊠ *Oxo Tower Wharf, Barge House Street, South Bank, SE1, 020/7803–3888.* U *Temple, Waterloo. £19–£35.*

The Place Below. Hit this atmospheric Norman crypt to find, of all things, a cheerful vegetarian restaurant. This is some of the best veggie cooking in the city; you might find spiced lentil soup, roast eggplant gratin, and mushroom and Stilton quiche on the

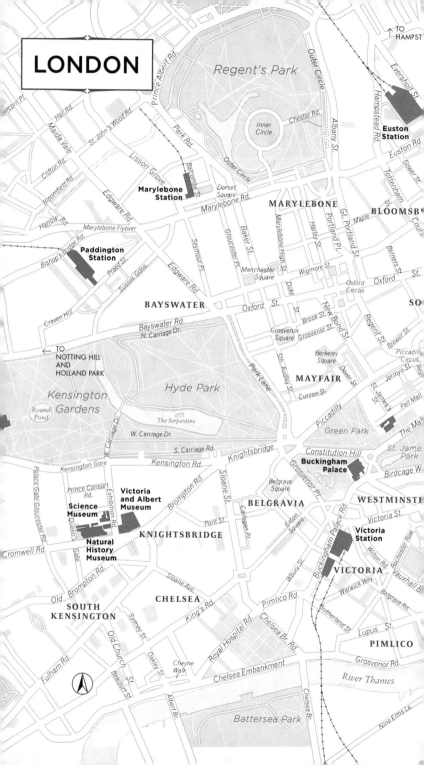

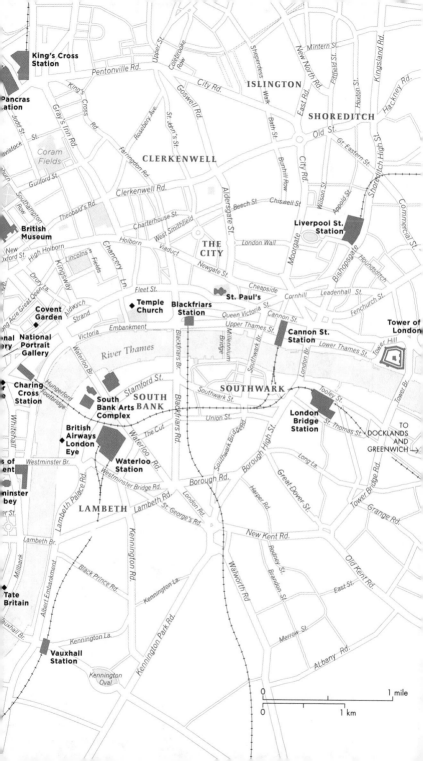

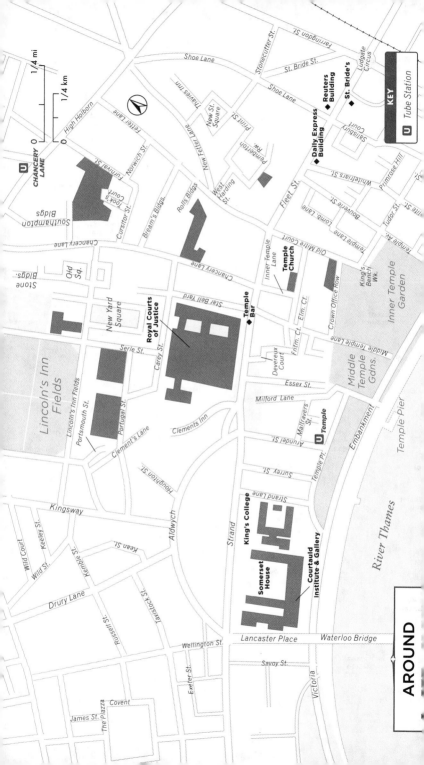

AROUND

KEY

U Tube Station

1/4 mi
1/4 km
0

CHANCERY LANE U

Southampton Bldgs

High Holborn

Tooke's Court
Cursitor St.
Norwich St.
Furnival St.
Chancery Lane

Fetter Lane
Thavies Inn
Shoe Lane
Stonecutter St.
Farringdon St.

New St. Square
Print St.
New Fetter Lane
Pemberton Row
West Harding St.

Shoe Lane
St. Bride St.
Ludgate Circus

♦ Reuters Building
♦ Daily Express Building
■ St. Bride's

Salisbury Court

Stone Bldgs

Old Sq.

New Yard Square

Serle St.

Carey St.
Star Bell Yard

Bream's Bldgs.
Rolls Bldgs.
Chancery Lane

Royal Courts
of Justice

Inner Temple Lane
Temple Church
♦ Temple Bar

Elm Ct.
Crown Office Row

Fleet St.
Bouverie St.
Temple Lane
Whitefriars St.
Primrose Hill

Old Mitre Court
Lombard Lane
King's Bench Wk.
Temple Av.

Lincoln's Inn
Fields

Lincoln's Inn Fields
Portsmouth St.
Portugal St.

Clement's Lane
Clements Inn

Fntm. Ct.
Devereux Court
Essex St.
Milford Lane

Inner Temple
Garden

Middle Temple Lane
Middle Temple Gdns.

Kingsway

Wild Court
Keeley St.
Kemble St.
Kean St.
Wild St.
Tavistock St.
Russell St.

Drury Lane

Aldwych
Houghton St.

Strand

Strand Lane
Temple Pl.
Surrey St.
Arundel St.
Maltravers St.

U Temple

Embankment

Temple Pier

King's College

Somerset House

Courtauld
Institute & Gallery

Lancaster Place   Waterloo Bridge

Wellington St.
Exeter St.
Savoy St.
Victoria

James St.
The Piazza
Covent

River Thames

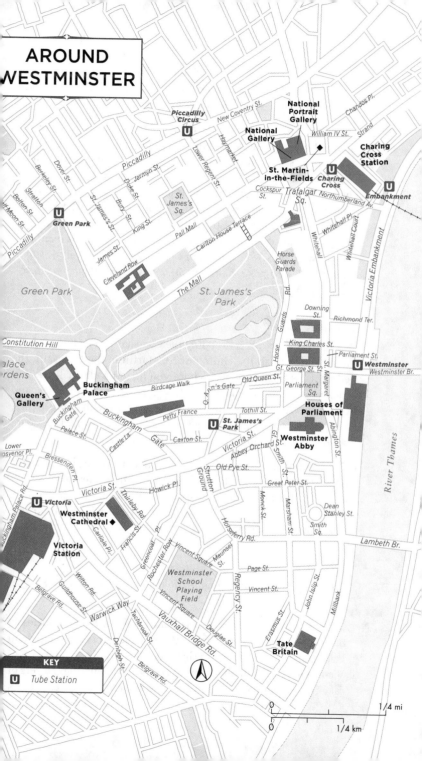

menu. It's an unusual and intriguing place to relax over breakfast or lunch. ⊠ *St. Mary Le Bow Church, Cheapside, St. Paul's, EC2, 020/7329–0789.* Ⓤ *St. Paul's. £5–£13.*

Shepherd's. Close to Westminster Abbey and the Houses of Parliament, this traditional English restaurant is a favorite of parliamentarians—so much so that a division bell, which alerts members to an impending vote on the floor, has been installed here. The look is legal chic, with lots of leather, polished wood, and, lest anyone get too pompous, political cartoons. The menu includes classics such as crab and brandy soup and roast grouse. For dessert, it has to be Eton mess (cream, fruit, and ice-cream in a gooey, well, mess). ⊠ *Marsham Court, Marsham Street, Westminster, SW1P, 020/7834–9552.* Ⓤ *St. James's Park, Pimlico. £26.50–£29.50 prix fixe.*

Quick Bites

Café in the Crypt. If decoding the *Code* has you feeling peckish, make a detour to the church of St.-Martin-in-the-Fields, on the edge of Trafalgar Square, where you'll find a clever little café tucked away in the cool crypt. Cakes, pastries, sandwiches, and coffee are sold in this surprisingly airy space with stone arches. ⊠ *Church of St.-Martin-in-the-Fields, Trafalgar Square, WC2, 020/7766–1129.* Ⓤ *Charing Cross Road, Embankment.*

The Cinnamon Bar. This gorgeous modern coffee bar in a chic hotel is just a few minutes' walk from the Middle Temple. Stop for any sort of pick-me-up: an espresso, sandwich, tea, pastry, or a glass of wine. ⊠ *One Aldwych Hotel, 1 Aldwych, at the Strand, Covent Garden, 020/7300–0800.* Ⓤ *Temple.*

Where to Stay

Quoted prices are for a standard double room in high season, 17.5% tax included.

Jolly Hotel St. Ermin's. This handy hotel with the hopelessly bad name is a short stroll from Westminster Abbey, Buckingham Palace, and the Houses of Parliament. The lobby is a showcase of Victorian baroque, with glittering crystal chandeliers and layers of cake-frosting stucco-work in baby blue and creamy white. The 285 guest rooms are nicely appointed, though some are quite small. Book online for discounts. ⊠ *2 Caxton Street, Westminster SW1. 020/7222–7888, www.jollyhotels.it.* Ⓤ *Westminster. £150–£320.*

Renaissance Chancery Court. This landmark building near Middle Temple is a fine home away from home for those with Teabing-like tastes. It seems an entire quarry was used for the marble staircase, bathrooms, and public spaces, and the attention to detail would satisfy even the fussiest guests. The spacious rooms balance good taste (well-chosen antiques and impressive reproductions) with modern luxury (up-to-the-minute amenities). The occasional Internet price discounts are substantial. ⊠ *252 High Holborn, Holborn WC1, 020/7829–9888. www. renaissancehotels.com.* Ⓤ *Holborn. £230–£350.*

The Rubens Hotel. *Code* chasers will love this inviting auberge overlooking the Royal Mews of Buckingham Palace. Elegant but not overdone, the hotel offers plenty of creature comforts—cushy armchairs, soft lighting, and a nice cup of tea near the fireplace. The 159 rooms are spacious and cozy, with dark floral fabrics, brass beds, and throw pillows. Modern touches include personal CD libraries in guestrooms, DVDs for adults and kids, and high-speed Internet access. Prices are quite reasonable, and you can't beat the location. ⊠ *38 Buckingham Palace Road, Westminster, SW1W 0PS, 020/7834–6600. www.rubenshotel.com.* Ⓤ *Charing Cross, Green Park. £168–£198.*

Sanctuary House. With a name likely to warm the hearts of *Da Vinci Code* fans, this pub hotel is just a short stroll from Westminster Abbey and Parliament. The 34 rooms are simple but not unstylish, and some have king-size four-poster beds. The Victorian pub downstairs is a mellow place with a good menu—ideal for an inexpensive lunch. This is a favorite with business travelers on a budget and tourists in the know, so book well in advance. The Sanctuary is near St. James's Park, where you can prowl for desiccated art connoisseurs and nefarious butlers. ⊠ *33 Tothill Street, Westminster SW1H 9LA, 020/7799–4044. www.sanctuaryhousehotel. com.* Ⓤ *St. James's Park. £99–£150.*

The Savoy. Does this grand hotel near the Middle Temple measure up to its lovingly cultivated reputation? Absolutely. All 263 guest rooms are impeccably maintained, spacious, and eminently

Code-Theme Walking Tours

*T*he following companies offer *Da Vinci Code* walking tours. Walks usually last about two hours.

■ **Original London Walks** (020/7624–3978, www.walks.com). Four "Blue Badge guides" lead *Code*-tinged, Monday afternoon tours of Westminster Abbey that focus on the sculpture, paintings, history, and architecture of the cathedral. A Wednesday afternoon walk hits more *Code* sights and investigates the "high strangeness" in other London landmarks.

■ **Golden Tours** (020/7233–7030, www.goldentours.co.uk). One

walking tour option focuses on Temple Church and the Knights Templar. Another walk heads to Westminster Abbey, where guides hold forth on Leonardo and examine some of the controversial ideas put forth about him in *The Da Vinci Code.*

Hitting Fleet Street.

comfortable. A room facing the Thames costs a fortune, but the views are worth it. Newer rooms are even larger and have vast bathrooms. The Savoy Grill is famous for its high prices and creative British cuisine (the kitchen works wonders with steak and kidney pie), and the new Banquette Restaurant is a chic turn on American diners, only here the burgers come with pear chutney. ⊠ *Strand, Covent Garden, WC2R 0EU, 020/7836–4343. www. fairmont.com/savoy/.* Ⓤ *Charing Cross. £300–£330.*

Places to See & Shop

Abbey Bookshop. Westminster Abbey's official gift shop has books on everything from the abbey's fascinating history to British royalty. You'll also find plenty of hard-to-find special-interest titles. A good resource for those doing further research into the history behind *The Da Vinci Code.* ⊠ *Westminster Abbey, 20 Deans Yard, Westminster, SW1, 020/7654–4920.* Ⓤ *Westminster.*

Covent Garden Antiques Market. Every Monday, dozens of independent antiques dealers from around the country converge on Covent Garden to sell an eclectic range of antique jewelry, silver, art, and fabrics, much of it from the 17th and 18th centuries. The buzzing flea-market atmosphere makes shopping here a memorable experience. ✉ *Covent Garden Piazza, Covent Garden, 020/ 7836–2139, www.jmh.company.org.uk.* Ⓤ *Covent Garden, Charing Cross.*

London Silver Vaults. A short walk from the Middle Temple, and protected by thick security doors, this extraordinary place has one of the world's largest collections of antique silver, including Italian pieces dating back to Leonardo's day. The vaults hold more than a dozen independent silver dealers, each with a different specialty, from early English silver to European and Asian pieces. ✉ *Chancery House, 53–64 Chancery Lane, Temple, WC2, 020/ 7242–3844. www.thesilvervaults.com.* Ⓤ *Chancery Lane, Temple.*

National Gallery. No trip to London is complete without a stop at one of the world's greatest art museums, and fans of the *Code* should be particularly eager to pay a visit. The vast collection includes no end of cream-of-the-crop daubs, from early Renaissance gems by Bellini to late 19th-century pointillist masterpieces by Seurat. *Code*sters should make a beeline to the Sainsbury Wing, a relatively recent addition by architect Robert Venturi, to see Leonardo's *Virgin of the Rocks* and the *Burlington House Cartoon,* depicting the Virgin and Child with Saint Anne. Hung nearby are Caravaggio's *Supper at Emmaus*, the divinely feminine *Venus and Mars* by Botticelli, and Velázquez's *The Toilet of Venus.* This is also where you can find some of the greatest Titians on earth, including the magnificently astral *Bacchus and Ariadne.* The museum's gift shop carries plenty of prints and art books, and also offers a custom poster service. You can choose any painting in the Gallery's collection and have a poster copy made on the spot. ✉ *Trafalgar Square, WC2, 020/7747–2885, www.nationalgallery.org.uk.* Ⓤ *Charing Cross, Embankment.*

National Portrait Gallery. This unusual institution devoted to British mugs is more exciting than it sounds. Unless you're a professional historian, many of the kissers will mean absolutely nothing to you, but there are also plenty of familiar faces, from Henry

VIII to Jane Austen to John Profumo. Among the snapshots of icons of cool are Mick Jagger, Madonna (recent vintage), and Jude Law. *Code* geeks will want to check out the portraits of Sirs Isaac Newton and Christopher Wren, green thumb André Le Nôtre, and supposed Priory of Sion Grand Masters Victor Hugo, Jean Cocteau, and Robert Boyle. Sorry, no pictures of Dan Brown. ⊠ *St. Martins Place, Trafalgar Square WC2, 020/7312–2463, www.npg.org.uk.* Ⓤ *Charing Cross, Leicester Square.*

Somerset House Gallery Shop. This peaceful shopping oasis, a five-minute walk from the Middle Temple, has art prints, glittering Renaissance-style jewelry, stationery, and writing implements. The shop is inside Somerset House, and is connected to the Courtauld Institute of Art. ⊠ *Somerset House, Strand, WC2, 020/7848–2579.* Ⓤ *Temple.*

Stanfords. You'll find travel books about virtually every corner of the globe here, in addition to an unmatched collection of books about London. Looking for a map of Roslin? It's here, along with maps of every country and city—no matter the size—on earth. ⊠ *12–14 Long Acre, Covent Garden, WC2, 020/7836–1321, www. stanfords.co.uk.* Ⓤ *Covent Garden.*

Where to Raise a Glass

Also see the Bottoms Up sidebar in the London & Roslin chapter.

Gordon's Wine Bar. The look of the place hasn't changed since World War II; there's still blackout paper on the few windows and in the yellowed press clippings on the walls the Queen is still young and rosy-cheeked. The low-ceilinged brick vault is lit entirely by candles, which are replaced by the energetic staff as they burn down. You order wine (and only wine) from a menu on the rickety counter. Prices are reasonable and the atmosphere unmatched. ⊠ *47 Villiers Street, Trafalgar Square, WC2N, 020/7930–1408.* Ⓤ *Embankment, Charing Cross.*

Jerusalem Tavern. According to lore, crusading knights gathered here for libations before heading out for the Continent. Other swells who've bellied up to the bar over the centuries include George Frederic Handel, Samuel Johnson, and Oliver Goldsmith.

It's a short cab ride from the Middle Temple. ✉ *55 Britton Street, Clerkenwell, EC1, 020/7490–4281.* Ⓤ *Farringdon.*

Knights Templar. Ceilings soar 25 feet above mosaic floors and the walls are decorated with knights on horseback at this vast pub with a Templar theme. It's not the coziest of places (and it's pretty smoky) but the nonsmoking library rooms at the back, with shelves of books and tables clustered around fireplaces, are more intimate. The bathrooms downstairs are rather decadent, with swinging curved doors and luxurious sofas in the ladies' room. ✉ *95 Chancery Lane, Holborn, WC2, 020/7831–2660.* Ⓤ *Temple, Chancery Lane.*

The Seven Stars. This tiny pub near the Middle Temple opened for business in 1602. It still has original features like a simple wooden frontage and crooked, low-beamed ceiling. You can get a simple meal, though sitting down to eat might be a problem, as there aren't many tables in the place. Most of the customers are attorneys from the courts across the street, so you can get all the legal gossip as they down Suffolk Cyder and Bitburger beer. ✉ *53–54 Carey Street, off Chancery Lane, Temple, WC2, 020/ 7242–8521.* Ⓤ *Temple, Chancery Lane.*

ROSLIN

Phone numbers are listed below with their local area codes. When dialing from abroad, drop the initial "0" from the local area code. The country code for Great Britain is 44. Great Britain is five hours ahead of Eastern Standard Time.

How to Get There

Roslin, six miles south of Edinburgh, is easily reached by bus or car. From the Edinburgh ring road, take Straiton Junction /A701 to Penicuik/Peebles. Follow the A701 for about three miles until you reach Roslin, a tiny village whose hotels and shops are clustered on the main street, which is also the center of town. A small sign off the main street indicates the turn-off to the chapel. The sign is covered in ivy and is easy to miss, but just follow the tour buses or the succession of black taxis turning on the road. If you'd rather take a bus from Edinburgh, both Lothian Buses (0131/555–6363 www.lothianbuses.co.uk) and First buses (www.firstgroup.com) offer service to Roslin. Lothian Bus service 15A (not the 15) departs from St. Andrew Square, Princes Street, or Lothian Road in Edinburgh. Or you can take a number 62 First bus from North Bridge along the Royal Mile.

Where to Eat

Quoted prices are per person for a main course at dinner, or the equivalent.

The restaurant pickings are slim in Roslin, since tourism here is a relatively new thing. Note to budding entrepreneurs: set up a small café here and you'll do well given the tour buses streaming through town.

Café at Rosslyn Chapel. The interior of Rosslyn Chapel is often several degrees colder than the outside temperature, so warm up with a mug of tea or coffee at the in-house café. Food is not served, so be sure to fuel up elsewhere in advance, or pack a snack. The café occupies a corner of the room, which also makes up the gift shop and chapel entrance. If you want to rest your legs there are a few chairs. ⊠ *Roslin, Midlothian, 0131/440–2159. £1–£4.*

The Original Rosslyn Inn. In need of some stick-to-the-ribs victuals before heading off to the chapel? The kitchen here serves up hearty pub grub—fish and chips, burgers, sandwiches, pints—in a dining room with drawings of Rosslyn Chapel. If the weather's nice, grab a table outside. ⊠ *4 Main Street, Roslin, Midlothian, 0131/440–2384. £8–£20.*

Roslin Glen Hotel. The Roslin Glen Hotel is the other major hotel in town, and although not as atmospheric as the Original, it's the only other option in town for a hot meal. The hotel serves lunch and dinner, and visitors can choose from poached salmon, fish and chips, or the classic haggis, served with neeps and tatties (turnips and mashed potatoes). ⊠ *2 Penicuik Road, Roslin, Midlothian, 0131/440–2029. £6–£21.*

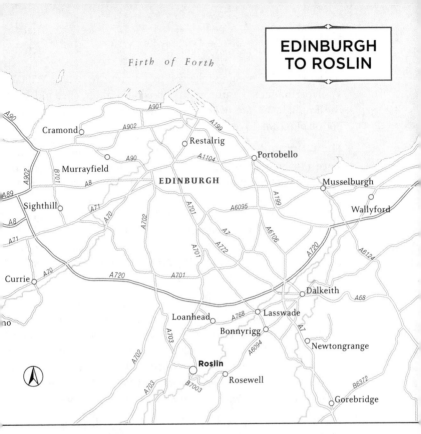

Where to Stay

Collegehill House. Sophie and Langdon visit a fieldstone house, near Rosslyn Chapel, where Sophie's grandmother lives. Although that house doesn't exist, the closest thing to the book's fictional cottage may be Collegehill House. This former inn was used as the gatehouse entrance to the chapel, so it's a mere few feet away from the church, which can be seen from some of the rooms. Queen Victoria, Robbie Burns, and J.M. Turner have all stayed at the inn, which sleeps six. The spacious rooms have a Scottish country feel, with tartan curtains and overstuffed chairs. ⊠ *Roslin, Midlothian. 0162/882–5925, www.landmarktrust.org.uk. £330–£975 a week.*

Gorton House. Here is a fine collection of cottages in Roslin Glen, a nature reserve bordering Roslin. The three individual cottages with barbecues offer the most privacy, but the rooms in the farmhouse have a casual country feel, with scrubbed pine floors and whitewashed furniture. In the mood for sleuthing? Ask owner Quintin Young to take you to a secret cave where William Wallace, the famed 13th-century freedom fighter, once hid from the English. ✉ *Lasswade, Midlothian, 0131/440–4332, www. gorton.plus.com. £450–£650 a week.*

The Original Rosslyn Inn. This full-service hotel, in business since 1857, has a busy bar, a dining room, and a room for private parties. There are plenty of nice touches, like the stone exterior walls and the exposed beams in the dining room, and the seven bedrooms are decorated in typical Scottish bed-and-breakfast style, with floral wallpaper and bedspreads. The rooms could use some spiffing up, but the hotel, in the center of Roslin village, is a good base for sightseeing. ✉ *4 Main Street, Roslin, Midlothian, 0131/440–2384. £60–£85 per person.*

Rosslyn Castle. The castle is deep in the woods, reachable by a winding path near the church's cemetery. It's an undeniably atmospheric setting—besides the woods, there's a 60-foot cliff down to the River Esk. The rooms, although spacious, are more modest than you'd expect, with wood-paneled walls and ubiquitous tartan upholstery. (The castle sleeps seven.) ✉ *Roslin, Midlothian, 0162/ 882–5925, www.landmarktrust.org.uk. £698–£1,798 a week.*

The Steading. Across the road from Rosslyn Chapel is this beautifully landscaped bed-and-breakfast, which was once a dairy farm. Its two simply furnished bedrooms—once cow sheds—are clean and comfortable, with new carpets and floral curtains. The owners are avid gardeners and the expansive grounds are bursting with exotic flowers and herbs. ✉ *Chapel Loan, Roslin, Midlothian, 0131/440–1608, www.roslin.org.uk. £27–£40 per person.*

Where to Raise a Glass

Acanthus. You can't miss this pub. The purple walls are one of the first things you'll see if you arrive in Edinburgh via Waverley Station. Its logo, on the exterior, is a large winged eye, often seen in Egyptian art. The namesake acanthus, a type of shrub, symbolizes heaven in Christian art. You can mull over these symbological factoids while making a dent in the extensive cocktail list. ✉ *17 Waverley Bridge, Old Town, Edinburgh, 0131/556–2358.*

The Beehive Inn. Langdon uses the ratio of female to male bees in a beehive as an example of PHI, also known as the Divine Proportion (1.618). You can ponder the possibilities while sipping pints here at the bar, which is dark and crowded but atmospheric—and rumored to be haunted by a ghost. Pub lunches are served, and many literary pub crawls start from here. ⊠ *18–20 Grassmarket, Grassmarket, Edinburgh, 0131/225–7171.*

Café Royal Circle Bar. Leonardo da Vinci placed his *Vitruvian Man* inside a circle, and Louvre curator Jacques Saunière pays homage to Leonardo's iconic image before dying. The Café Royal Circle Bar features a (you guessed it) circle-shaped bar. One wall is covered with eight-foot-high tiles by John Eyre depicting various inventors, including English chemist and physicist Michael Faraday. The bar's wine list is extensive and you can nosh on classic Scottish fare with a twist. ⊠ *17 West Register Street, New Town, Edinburgh, 0131/ 556–1884.*

Places to Shop

Edinburgh Crystal. In the nearby town of Penicuik, Edinburgh Crystal has been producing fine glassware for centuries. The designs have mystical names such as Eclipse, Orbit, Storm, and Energis. If you're watching your dollars, factory seconds are also available. ⊠ *Eastfield, Penicuik (just off A701 to Peebles, and a few miles south of Roslin), 0196/867–5128.*

Geoffrey (Tailor) Kiltmakers. Want to tour Rosslyn Chapel in an authentic Sinclair tartan? Rent a kilt from Geoffrey (Tailor) Kiltmakers. The shop has supplied kilts for the likes of Robbie Williams and Mel Gibson. If it's funky you want, try something from the 21st Century Kilt line, which includes leather and denim kilts. ⊠ *57–59 High Street, Royal Mile, Edinburgh, 0131/557–0256.*

Rosslyn Chapel Gift Shop. Where else could you buy Les Templiers wine, created by a group of Knights Templar in France? The gift shop is chock full of knickknacks drawing on gargoyles, Green Men (a pagan symbol of fertility and rebirth), and zodiac symbols. You can snap up plaster replicas of the Apprentice Pillar and homemade Rosslyn Chapel–branded jams and jellies. The shop also has a good selection of books on everything from codes to conspiracy theories. ⊠ *Roslin, Midlothian, 0131/440–2159.*

ON THE ROAD WITH *THE DA VINCI CODE*

Index

About Our Writers

Editors Jennifer Paull and Christopher Culwell would like to thank Bethany Beckerlegge, Vanessa Berberian, Candice Chaplin, Paul Eisenberg, Tim Jarrell, Peter Kay, Tina Malaney, Melanie Marin, Kristen Moehlmann, David Naggar, Jacinta O'Halloran, John Rambow, and Will Wu for their outstanding efforts and many a laugh. Thanks also to the helpful staffs of Westminster Abbey, Temple Church, the Louvre, and Rosslyn Chapel.

Isabel Allen is a New Englander in Paris who writes about art history, culture, and cuisine. *St-Sulpice, Château Villette.*

Ferne Arfin is a London-based writer whose travel writing has appeared in London's *Financial Times,* the *Boston Globe,* and *The New York Times. Temple Church, The Temple, Templar History.*

Elizabeth Bard is a journalist and art historian living in Paris. Her work has appeared in *The New York Times, Wired,* and *Time Out.* She is also a guide for Paris Muse. *The Louvre, Arc du Carrousel.*

Jacqueline Brown has lived in London for more than 20 years and is the author of *Fodor's Around London with Kids. Westminster Abbey, Sir Christopher Wren, St. James's Park, Fleet Street.*

Christi Daugherty is a Texas native contentedly out of place in England, where she works as a writer and editor of travel books. Her work has appeared in, among other publications, the *London Times* and the *Financial Times.* In her spare time she is writing a mystery novel. *London travel recommendations, London's Opus Dei headquarters.*

Michelle Delio is a New York–based freelance writer who has written extensively on arts, tattooing, technology, and travel. *Priory of Sion, cryptexes, Mary Magdalene, the* Codex Leicester, *Leonardo's codes, interviews with Martin Kemp and Bob Currie.*

Erica Firpo writes about culture and travel from her home in Rome, where she is also a tour guide specializing in art history. She has also written the self-published dining guide to Rome, *Little Black Book Rome. The Vatican, infamous popes, Rome travel recommendations.*

Leslie Fuller is a multiple-Emmy-award–winning writer and producer for television and public radio. She is the co-originator of the popular NPR series "Wait Wait Don't Tell Me." She is currently staff writer for the Hallmark Channel's series "New Morning." *Dead Sea Scrolls and Nag Hammadi Library.*

Adam Gold is a London native. He writes and edits for publications throughout the U.K. and, in between frequent travels abroad, can often be found on a London soccer field. *King's College, Fleet Street pubs.*

James Gracie is a travel writer who focuses on Scotland, his home country. He has written many guidebooks (including the *Country Living Guide to Rural Scotland*) and articles, mainly for the *Herald, Sunday Herald, Scots Magazine* and *The Highlander. Rosslyn Chapel.*

Lisa Pasold grew up in Montreal, which gave her the necessary jay-walking skills to survive in Paris. She currently lives behind Montmartre, where she writes about her favorite city and gives walking tours. *The Tuileries, Champs-Elysées, Gare St-Lazare, Bois de Boulogne.*

Mathew Schwartz is a globe-trotting freelance writer and photographer who lived in Paris and environs for several years. His writing has appeared in such publications as *The Times of London* and *Wired News.* His Police Judiciare experiences are purely in a research capacity. *The Ritz Paris, the Police Judiciare.*

Will Shank is an independent curator and conservator based in the San Francisco Bay Area. Formerly Chief Conservator at the San Francisco Museum of Modern Art, and the winner of the 2005 Rome Prize in Conservation, he writes about culture for the *Bay Area Reporter, The Advocate,* and London's *The Art Newspaper.* The Last Supper *and its conservation, Caravaggio, Castel Gandolfo.*

Laura Smith Kay has written for *Entertainment Weekly, People, Teen People* and *Bon Appetit.* She and her family live in New York City. *Constantine and early Christianity.*

Heather Stimmler-Hall is a Paris-based guidebook author, tour guide, and editor of the *Secrets of Paris* newsletter. She has encyclopedic knowledge of the city's streets and precise coordinates of the best public restrooms. *Paris travel recommendations.*

Jessica Teisch, author of *Da Vinci for Dummies,* holds a Ph.D. in geography. She currently serves as Managing Editor of *Bookmarks* magazine and works in Berkeley. *Leonardo's life and times.*

Christina Valhouli is a London-based freelance travel writer whose work has appeared in *The New York Times, Town & Country, Four Seasons* magazine, and *The New York Post.* She was married in Rosslyn Chapel in July 2005, but none of her guests managed to break the code. *Roslin travel recommendations.*

ABOUT OUR PHOTOGRAPHER

Photographer **Vanessa Berberian,** a Boston native based in London, travels regularly around Europe on assignment for travel guides and magazines. Her pictures have appeared in publications such as *British Tatler* and *Good Housekeeping.* Among her other clients are Getty Images, the British Luxury Council, the London Business School, and award-winning event designer Matt James. Her work may also be seen on her Web site, www.photopathos.com.

PHOTO CREDITS

All photos are by Vanessa Berberian unless otherwise noted.

INTRODUCTION *1, Mona Lisa,* Réunion des Musées Nationaux/Art Resource. *2 (top left),* Leonardo's *The Vitruvian Man,* Cameraphoto/Art Resource, NY. *2 (middle left),* St-Sulpice. *2 (bottom left),* Château Villette. *2 (top center),* members of the DCPJ. *2 (bottom center),* Arago plaque in the Palais Royal. *3 (top left),* Tuileries Gardens. *3 (top right),* SmartCar. *3 (bottom),* Palais Royal. *4–5 (top),* Leonardo's study for *The Last Supper,* red chalk drawing, Alinari/Art Resource. *4–5 (bottom),* Andy Warhol's *The Last Supper* (1986), The Andy Warhol Foundation, Inc./Art Resource, NY. *6 (top left),* King's College. *6 (top right),* The Temple. *6 (bottom),* Temple Church. *7 (top left),* image of Templar Grand Master Jacques de Molay, Mary Evans Picture Library. *7 (top right),* Westminster Abbey. *7 (center right), Virgin of the Rocks,* detail of the angel, Réunion des Musées Nationaux/Art Resource. *7 (bottom right),* carvings from Rosslyn Chapel, Scotland. 8, Leonardo's study of the Virgin Mary for *Virgin and Child with St. Anne,* Alinari Archives/Corbis.

PARIS *13,* Tuileries Gardens. *14 (top left),* Ritz Paris suite, Ritz Paris. *14 (top center),* Arc du Carrousel. *14 (top right),* Bar Hemingway sign, Ritz Paris. *22 (top left),* La Grande Pyramide. *22 (top center),* the Louvre's Grand Gallery. *22 (top right),* the Louvre's Salle des Etats. *28,* portrait of Baron Dominique Vivant Denon (1808), Réunion des Musées Nationaux/Art Resource. *38, Virgin of the Rocks,* Réunion des Musées Nationaux/Art Resource. *40 (top left),* SmartCar. *40 (top center),* Château Villette. *40 (top right),* St-Sulpice. *41,* La Grande Pyramide. *42–43 (top),* La Grande Pyramide. *42–43 (bottom left),* construction work at the Louvre, Corbis. *42–43 (bottom center),* image of 1830 uprising, Mary Evans Picture Library. *42–43 (bottom right),* the Louvre's Galerie d'Apollon by Victor Duval, Christie's Images Ltd. *44–45 (top left),* the construction of La Grande Pyramide, 1986, Thierry Orban/Corbis. *44–45 (top center),* architect I.M. Pei stands in front of the construction site for the Louvre's inverted pyramid, Owen Franken/Corbis. *44–45 (top right),* Louvre's entrance hall. *44–45 (bottom),* La Grande Pyramide. *46,* the Louvre's Grand Gallery. *47,* Caravaggio's *Death of the Virgin,* Réunion des Musées Nationaux/Art Resource. *48 (top left),* member of the DCPJ. *48 (top center),* Ritz Paris. *49 (top left),* suite at the Ritz Paris, Ritz Paris. *49 (bottom),* Ritz Paris. *50 (top),* mug shot of Vincenzo Perugia, Corbis. *50 (bottom),* the Mona Lisa in the Louvre's Salle des Etats. *51, Mona Lisa,* Réunion des Musées Nationaux/Art Resource. *52, The Madonna of the Rocks,* the Louvre, Scala/Art Resource. *53, The Virgin of the Rocks,* the National Gallery, London, Art Resource, NY/Art Resource. *54–55,* Tuileries Gardens. *56,* Arc du Carrousel.

HISTORY LESSONS *71,* Leonardo's *The Last Supper,* after its most recent restoration, Erich Lessing. *72 (top left),* detail of Mary Magdalene from the *Virgin and Child with St. Catherine and Mary Magdalene* by Giovanni Bellini, the Bridgeman Art Library. *72 (top second from left),* the Scroll of the Rule, West Semitic Research/Dead Sea Scrolls Foundation/Corbis. *72 (top third from left),* bronze head of Constantine the

Great, 4th century, Scala/Art Resource. *72 (top right)*, a replica cryptex, Justin Nevins/cryptex.org. *86 (top)*, the Venus of Willendorf, Corbis. *86 (center)*, statue of Bast, Bridgeman Art Library. *86 (bottom)*, classical European statue of Athena, Corbis. *87 (top)*, Indian miniature of the Goddess Sarasvati, late 18th century, Jean-Louis Nou/akg-images. *87 (second)*, statue of Epona, Bridgeman Art Library. *87 (third)*, Qing Dynasty ivory sculpture of Kuan Yin, Corbis. *87 (bottom)*, image of Hel, Mary Evans Picture Library. *89*, an Arago disk in the Palais Royal. *90 (top)*, the Gare St-Lazare. *90 (bottom)*, a replica cryptex, Justin Nevins/cryptex.org. *91*, SmartCar. *92*, interior of the Eglise St-Sulpice. *93*, the obelisk and brass line in St-Sulpice. *94*, Château Villette. *96–97*, Leonardo's *The Last Supper*, after its most recent restoration, Erich Lessing. *98 (top)*, detail of Christ with St. John in *The Last Supper* by Barna da Siena, A.M. Rosati/Art Resource. *98 (bottom)*, *Last Supper* by Jacopo Bassano, Cameraphoto Arte, Venice Art Resource. *99 (top)*, *The Last Supper* by Tintoretto, Cameraphoto/Art Resource. *99 (bottom)*, *The Last Supper*, detail from the Silver Treasury of Santissima Annunziata, by Fra Angelico, Bridgeman Art Library. *100 (top left)*, polychrome black Madonna, 17th century, Erich Lessing/Art Resource. *100 (top right)*, Saintes-Maries-de-la-Mer festival, France, Chris Lisle/Corbis. *100 (bottom)*, detail of Mary washing the feet of Christ from the *Life of Saint Mary Magdalene* by Giotto, Corbis. *101*, *The Penitent Magdalene* by Georges de la Tour, Scala/Art Resource. *102–103*, the Palais Royal. *104*, the inverted pyramid in the Louvre.

LEONARDO: RENAISSANCE MAN *109*, Leonardo's study for the head of Leda, Scala/Art Resource. *110 (top left)*, Leonardo's drawing and architectural plan of a cathedral, Alinari Archives/Corbis. *110 (top center)*, Ginevra de' Benci by Leonardo da Vinci, The Art Archive. *110 (top right)*, flying machine sketch by Leonardo da Vinci, Art Resource, NY/Art Resource. *130*, *L.H.O.O.Q.*, Cameraphoto/Art Resource. *137*, Leonardo's *The Vitruvian Man*, Cameraphoto/Art Resource, NY. *138*, Leonardo's self-portrait, red chalk drawing, Scala/Art Resource. *139*, a page from Leonardo's treatise on water, Corbis. *140–141 (top)*, Castel Gandolfo, Will Shank. *140–141 (bottom)*, inside the Vatican Museums, Digital Vision/age fotostock. *142*, Leonardo's design for a fixed-wing aircraft, HIP/Art Resource, NY. *143*, glider built by Skysport Engineering, Martin Kimm/Skysport Engineering Ltd. *144 (top)*, Leonardo's study of the effects of light, Scala/Art Resource, NY. *144 (bottom)*, *Lady with an Ermine* by Leonardo da Vinci, Erich Lessing/Art Resource, NY.

ROME & THE VATICAN *145*, St. Peter's Basilica, Vatican City, SuperStock/age fotostock. *146 (top left and center)*, Castel Gandolfo, Will Shank. *146 (top right)*, St. Peter's Basilica, Vatican City, SuperStock/age fotostock.

LONDON & ROSLIN *153*, Westminster Abbey. *154 (top left and center)*, Temple Church. *154 (top right)*, Fleet Street pub. *172 (top left)*, reading room in King's College. *172 (top center)*, pelicans in St. James's Park. *172 (top right)*, Westminster Abbey. *177*, London skyline. *178*, Fleet Street. *179*, pubs on Fleet Street. *180 (top)*, garden in the Temple. *180 (bottom)*, entrance to the Temple. *181*, Temple Church. *182*, interior of Temple Church. *183 (top left and right)*, St. James's Park. *183 (bottom)*, effigy of a knight in Temple Church. *184*, reading room in King's College. *185*, Greenwich Observatory, Greenwich. *186–187*, Westminster Abbey. *188 (top left)*, Newton's Tomb. *188 (top right)*, College Garden. *189 (top)*, Chapter House. *189 (bottom)*, interior of Westminster Abbey. *190*, exterior of Rosslyn Chapel, Scotland. *191 (top)*, carved stonework, Rosslyn Chapel, Scotland. *191 (bottom)*, the Mason's Pillar, Journeyman's Pillar, and Apprentice Pillar, Rosslyn Chapel, Scotland. *192*, exterior of Rosslyn Chapel, Scotland. *195*, detail of Poet's Corner memorials, Westminster Abbey. *200*, carved stonework, Rosslyn Chapel, Scotland.

ON THE ROAD WITH THE DA VINCI CODE *207*, fountains in the Louvre courtyard. *208 (top left)*, Tuileries Gardens. *208 (top center)*, Palais Royal. *208 (top right)*, pub, London. *210*, Tuileries Gardens. *222*, Arago plaque. *240*, Fleet Street.

FODOR'S GUIDE TO *THE DA VINCI CODE*

Editors: Jennifer Paull and Christopher Culwell
Photographer: Vanessa Berberian
Designer: Tina Malaney
Creative Director: Fabrizio La Rocca
Editorial Production: Bethany Cassin Beckerlegge
Photo Editor and Archival Researcher: Melanie Marin
Maps and Plans: David Lindroth, *cartographer;* Mark Stroud, Moon Street Cartography; William Wu
Production/Manufacturing: Robert B. Shields

Cover Photos: *Mona Lisa,* Réunion des Musées Nationaux/Art Resource, NY; Pyramid, Terry Vine/Stone/Getty Images

First Edition
ISBN: 1-4000-1672-X
ISBN-13: 978-1-4000-1672-3
A catalog record for this title is available from the Library of Congress.

The details in this book are based on information supplied to us at press time, but changes occur all the time, and the publisher cannot accept responsibility for facts that become outdated or for inadvertent errors or omissions.

Fodor's Travel, 1745 Broadway, New York, NY 10019
PRINTED IN THE U.S.A.
10 9 8 7 6 5 4 3 2 1

Fodor's "Expedia Da Vinci Code Experience" Sweepstak

Relive your favorite moments from the novel with a 6~day/5~night Parisian excursion for you and a friend.

Fodor's
Open to legal residents of the 50 United States and the District of Columbia, who are 18 years of age or older as of March 28, 2006. Sweepstakes ends May 31, 2006.

Expedia.co

OFFICIAL RULES

NO PURCHASE NECESSARY. VOID IN PUERTO RICO AND WHERE PROHIBITED. TO ENTER:

MAIL-IN ENTRY:
Handprint your complete name and address, including zip code, and phone number (optional) on an Official Entry Form, 3" x 5" index card or piece of paper. Mail entry in a hand-addressed (#10) envelope to: Fodor's "Expedia DaVinci Code Experience" Sweepstakes, P.O. Box 878, Farmingdale, NY 11735. Entries must be postmarked by May 31, 2006 and received by June 9, 2006.

ONLINE ENTRY:
Enter online beginning at 12:00 Midnight, U.S. Eastern Time (ET) March 28, 2006 through 11:59 PM, U.S. Eastern Time (ET) May 31, 2006 at www.fodors.com/parissweepstakes by following the Fodor's "Expedia DaVinci Code Experience" Sweepstakes directions and providing your complete name, address and email address.

For All Entries: Limit one (1) entry per person, regardless of the method of entry used. Multiple entries from the same person and/or email address will be void. Entries become the exclusive property of Sponsor and will not be acknowledged or returned. By entering, you fully and unconditionally agree to these Official Rules and the decisions of Sponsor, which are final and binding.

Sponsor is not responsible for lost/late/misdirected entries or computer malfunctions. Entries that contain errors, are incomplete, corrupted or illegible will not be accepted. Sponsor reserves the right to disqualify entries from anyone tampering with the Internet entry process. Sponsor assumes no responsibility for any error, omission, interruption, deletion, defect, delay in operation or transmission, communications line failure, theft, destruction, or unauthorized access to the site.

WINNER SELECTION:
One (1) potential Grand Prize Winner will be selected in a random drawing from all eligible entries, conducted on or about June 20, 2006, by the Sponsor. Odds of winning depend on the number of eligible entries received. Potential Winner will be notified by mail on or about July 1, 2006. If Sponsor is unable to contact potential winner within seven (7) days of the first attempt to notify him/her, a new potential winner will be selected at random from among all remaining eligible entries.

PRIZE:
One (1) Grand Prize: An Expedia Da Vinci Code Experience Trip for two (2) to Paris, France. Trip consists of round-trip coach class air transportation for two (2); standard hotel accommodations for two (2) (One room, double occupancy) for six (6) days and five (5) nights; round trip ground transportation to/from Paris Charles de Gaulle Airport and the hotel; and at least one (1) activity for two (2), with total activity value up to $250. All carriers, hotel and prize providers are selected by Sponsor in its sole discretion. For more details on the Da Vinci Code Experience Trip, visit www.expedia.com/davinciexperience. (Approximate Retail Value of prize package: up to $5,000. Actual value will depend on location of the winner's residence and time of travel. Any difference between approximate and actual value will not be awarded.)

Items not specifically listed in the Grand Prize description above, including but not limited to added ground transportation, meals, drinks, snacks, room service, laundry, and all other personal and incidental expenses, will be solely Winner's responsibility. Winner must travel by July 1, 2007. Bookings must be made through Sponsor, and travel dates are subject to availability, blackout periods and restrictions. Once travel arrangements are made, no changes will be permitted. All travel must be from the major airport nearest to Winner's U.S. residence and Winner will be responsible for any travel to and from that airport. Winner and travel companion must travel on the same itinerary. No transfer or cash or other substitution of prize permitted, except by Sponsor, which reserves the right, in its sole discretion, to substitute a prize or prize component with another of comparable or greater value.

WHO CAN PARTICIPATE:
Open to legal residents of the 50 United States and the District of C(who are 18 years of age or older as of March 28, 2006. Employees of Travel, Random House, Inc., Expedia, Inc. and each of their respect ents, subsidiaries, affiliates and agencies, and the immediate family as spouse, children, parents and siblings) and persons living in th household of such employees are not eligible. Void in Puerto Rico an prohibited.

REQUIREMENTS OF POTENTIAL WINNER & GENERAL CONDITIONS
All taxes will be the responsibility of the Winner. Except where pr(potential Winner will be required to execute an Affidavit of Eligibl Publicity/Liability Release within 14 days of notification or prize forfeited and an alternate potential Winner selected. Winner's companion must be 18 years of age or older and must execute a Release within the same time period. Noncompliance with any cond result in disqualification and selection of an alternate potential Winner and traveling companion will be responsible for securing pa photo I.D., proof of citizenship or other travel documents required f national travel. Sweepstakes is subject to applicable laws and regul the U.S. By acceptance of prize, Winner agrees to Sponsor's use o name/likeness for commercial purposes without notification/compe except where prohibited by law. If, for any reason, the sweepstak drawing is not capable of running as planned as a result of a compu tampering, unauthorized intervention, fraud, technical limitations or or any other causes which, in the sole opinion of the Sponsc compromise, undermine or otherwise affect the Official Rules, admin security, fairness or proper conduct of the sweepstakes, the reserves the right to cancel terminate, modify or suspend the swee In the event of termination or cancellation, the Winners will be selec all eligible entries received before termination.

RELEASE & LIMITATION OF LIABILITY:
By participating in the Sweepstakes, entrants agree to release harmless Sponsor, Random House, Inc., Expedia, Inc., each of their re related companies, and each such company's officers, directors, er and agents (collectively, the "Released Parties") from and against a or cause of action arising out of participation in the Sweepstakes o or use of any prize, including, without limitation: (a) unauthorize intervention in the Sweepstakes; (b) technical or printing errors; (c)(the administration of the Sweepstakes or the processing of entries lost, misdirected or undeliverable mail; or (e) injury or da persons or property, including but not limited to death, which may be directly or indirectly, in whole or in part, from entrant's participat Sweepstakes or receipt or use of any prize. Entrants waive the righ any damages against the Released Parties whatsoever, including limitation, punitive, consequential or indirect damages. Entrants a that any and all disputes, claims and causes of action arising connected with the Sweepstakes or any prize awarded shall be individually, without resort to any form of class action.

TO OBTAIN THE NAME OF THE WINNER:
For the name of the Winner, available after August 1, 2006 self-addressed, stamped envelope to be received by December 31 Fodor's "Expedia DaVinci Code Experience" Sweepstakes, Fodor's division of Random House, Inc., 1745 Broadway, New York, NY 100 Attention: Marketing Department. Vermont residents may omit return

Promotion Sponsor is Fodor's Travel, a division of Random House, Broadway, New York, NY 10019.

Fodor's "Expedia Da Vinci Code Experience" Sweepstakes

Entries must be postmarked by May 31, 2006 and received by June 9, 2006. Entries must be hand-address and sent in an envelope (#10) to: Fodor's "Expedia DaVinci Code Experience" Sweepstakes, P.O. Box 878, Farmingdale, NY 11735, U.S.A. No purchase necessary.

Name: _____ Age: _____

Email: _____

Mailing Address: _____

Zip/Postal Code: _____ Phone: _____